T0043103

REWRITING OUR STORIES

Education, empowerment,
and well-being

To all of the storytellers –
which is everyone.
Our teachings create
better worlds.

MindYourSelf titles

Personal Struggles:
Oppression, healing and liberation

Uncertainty Rules?
Making uncertainty work for you

Also by **Derek Gladwin**

Contentious Terrains

Eco-Joyce

Ecological Exile

Gastro-Modernism

Unfolding Irish Landscapes

REWRITING OUR STORIES

Education, empowerment, and well-being

Dr Derek Gladwin

SERIES EDITOR: **Dr Marie Murray**

First published in 2021 by Atrium
Atrium is an imprint of Cork University Press
Boole Library
University College Cork
Cork T12 ND89
Ireland

Library of Congress Control Number: 2020934709

Distribution in the USA Longleaf Services, Chapel Hill,
NC, USA.

British Library Cataloguing in Publication Data
A CIP catalogue record for this book is available from the
British Library.

ISBN 9781782054177
Printed in Malta by Gutenberg Press
Typeset by Studio 10 Design

Cover image courtesy of shutterstock.com

www.corkuniversitypress.com

CONTENTS

DISCLAIMER

This book has been written for general readers to introduce the topic or to increase their knowledge and understanding of it. It is not intended, or implied, to be a substitute for professional consultation or advice in this, or allied, areas. Any content, text, graphics, images or other information provided in any of the *MindYourSelf* books is for general purposes only.

On topics that have medical, psychological, psychiatric, psychotherapy, nursing, physiotherapy, occupational therapy, educational, vocational, organisational, sociological, legal or any mental health- or physical health-related or other content, *MindYourSelf* books do not replace diagnosis, treatment, or any other appropriate professional consultations and interventions. This also applies to any information or website links contained in the book.

While every effort has been made to ensure the accuracy of the information in the book, it is possible that errors or omissions may occur. Research also leads to new multidisciplinary perspectives in all professional areas, so that, despite all the publishers' caution and care, new thinking on certain topics may alter the accuracy of the content. The authors, editors and publishers can, therefore, assume no responsibility, nor provide any guarantees or warranties concerning the up-to-date nature of the information provided.

DR MARIE MURRAY has worked as a clinical psychologist for more than forty years across the entire developmental spectrum. An honours graduate of UCD, from where she also obtained an MSc and PhD, she is a chartered psychologist, registered family therapist and supervisor, a member of both the Irish Council for Psychotherapy and the European Association for Psychotherapy as well as the APA American Psychological Association and a former member of the Heads of Psychology Services in Ireland. Key clinical posts have included being Director of Psychology in St Vincent's Psychiatric Hospital, Dublin, and Director of the Student Counselling Services in UCD. Marie served on the Medical Council of Ireland (2008–13) and on the Council of the Psychological Society of Ireland (2014–17). She has presented internationally, from the Tavistock and Portman NHS Trust in London, to Peking University, Beijing. She was an *Irish Times* columnist for eight years and has been author, co-author, contributor, and editor to a number of bestselling books, many with accompanying RTÉ radio programmes. Her appointment as Series Editor to the Cork University Press *MindYourSelf* series gathers a lifetime of professional experience to bring safe clinical information to general and professional readers.

MindYourSelf

Few expressions convey as much care as that lovely phrase 'mind yourself'. Quintessentially Irish, it is a blessing, an injunction, an endearment and a solicitous farewell. Like many simple phrases, 'mind yourself' has layers of psychological meaning, so that while it trips lightly off the tongue at the end of conversations, there are depths of kindness that accompany it.

Being told to 'mind yourself' touches the heart. It resonates with the longing in each of us to have somebody in our world who cares about us. Saying 'mind yourself' means 'you matter to me', that what happens to you is important, and may nothing bad befall you. It is a cautionary phrase, with a gentle acknowledgement of your personal responsibility in self-care. Although it has become so ingrained in our leave-taking that we may not consciously note it, unconsciously, being minded is an atavistic need in all of us. 'Mind yourself' is what parents say to children, to adolescents, what people say to each other, to family and friends. We also say it to reassure ourselves that we have reminded those we love to keep themselves safe.

It is in this spirit of recognising the importance of self-care that the *MindYourSelf* book series has been designed; to bring safe, researched, peer-reviewed information from front-line professionals to help people to mind themselves. While, at one level, information – about everything – is now on multiple platforms at the touch of a screen, relying on internet sites is a problem. What is true? Whom can you trust? How do you sift through the data to find what you need to know? Because it is not lack of access to facts, but fact overload, that makes people increasingly conscious of the dangers of misinformation, contradictory perspectives, internet prognoses, and the risk of unreliable or exploitative sources. What people want is simply the information that is relevant to them, delivered by professionals who care about their specialities and who are keen to help readers understand the topic. May this Cork University Press *MindYourSelf* series find its way to all who need it, and give readers the tools and resources to really mind themselves.

Dr Marie Murray, Series Editor, *MindYourSelf*

Praise for *Rewriting Our Stories*

'Narrative theory has inspired an exciting and effective array of professional practices over the years – in education, therapy, healthcare, organizational development and beyond. With clarity, wisdom, and care, Derek Gladwin now makes the riches of a narrative perspective available for the practice of everyday life. We should all be grateful.'

– Kenneth Gergen, PhD, social psychologist, president of The Taos Institute, and author of *An Invitation to Social Construction* and *Relational Being: Beyond Self and Community*

'Dr. Gladwin has done a fabulous job at having us examine and heal our stories. Our stories create our prisons and we are the only ones who can free ourselves. In this easy to read, and interactive book, you will truly re-write your story. You will dive headfirst into a journey that will heal, open you up and change your life forever.'

– Divi Chandna, MD, Director of the Center of Mind Body Spirit Medicine and author of *You Don't Look Psychic: Your Essential Guide to Tapping into your Natural Powers*

'We tell stories, but our stories also tell us, and in ways that we are usually completely unconscious or unaware of. Sometimes, moreover, we may not be served, much less saved, by these stories telling us. We might be held back, blinded, made afraid, even harmed and rendered sick and hateful. So why not change these stories? Why not just tell a different story to and as ourselves? This is the hopeful, practical, and fundamentally positive message of Derek Gladwin, a skilled translator and trustworthy guide through a mountain of technical research

in psychology, literature, history, religion, and philosophy—
in short, a storyteller of storytellers.'

– Jeffrey J. Kripal, PhD, J. Newton Rayzor Chair in philosophy
and religious thought at Rice University and author of *The
Flip: Epiphanies of Mind and the Future of Knowledge*

'Dr. Derek Gladwin has written a life-affirming guide to an
internal revolution by revealing the power of stories to shape
our imagination, relationships, and possible futures.'

– Nisha Sajnani, PhD, director of the Drama Therapy Program
and professor at New York University

'Based on the simple assumption that "words create worlds,"
Rewriting Our Stories challenges readers to change their lives
by changing their stories. It is full of ideas for how to transform stories of fear, failure, struggle and scarcity into stories
and experiences of acceptance and gratitude. It is a book for
students of all ages, for anyone wanting to understand how
they keep themselves stuck in downward cycles of fear, and for
everyone wishing to create a better life.'

– Diana Whitney, PhD, co-founder of The Taos Institute,
founder and director emeritus of the Corporation for Positive
Change, and author of *Appreciative Inquiry, Appreciative Leadership, and Thriving Women Thriving World*

'A high level of well-being constitutes a meaningful goal for
people across all sectors of society. Well-being reflects how
people evaluate and experience their lives and their life conditions, and is inherently linked to freedom, mastery and
meaning in life, to positive emotions, social connection
and well-functioning, to health and mortality. Dr Gladwin's

inspiring and important book *Rewriting Our Stories: Education, empowerment and well-being* invites us to take a relationally responsible approach to co-construct well-being communities and relationships for a sustainable society based on challenging and rewriting our stories towards well-being for all! A must-read and world timely book! Read, reflect and act!'

– Ottar Ness, PhD, professor of education and lifelong learning at Norwegian University of Science and Technology

'Derek Gladwin's book is a timely and welcome arrival in a time of great uncertainty. In a warm and candid manner, Gladwin helps us see the ways in which the stories that we tell ourselves keep us bound by belief systems that reinscribe hierarchies and make us feel hopeless or scared. We have the capacity, Gladwin tells us, to retell these stories, and in so doing reshift our perceptions. This is no ordinary self-care book. Rather, it is an approachable analysis of societal ills, and offers a new way of thinking about that oldest of practices—storytelling—in order to reshape the social forces around us. Gladwin explains political and cultural systems easily and clearly, so that readers of all different backgrounds can connect to his message. As he says, "We all rewrite the stories that eventually transform our collective stories, without fully understanding their potential impacts. This is the point: we must do storying; we must be our stories." In the intimate, vulnerable, and open writing of this book, Gladwin has not only "done storying" but also given us the tools to begin to be our own stories.'

– Eva-Lynn Jagoe, PhD, professor of comparative literature at University of Toronto, author of *Take Her, She's Yours*, and Iyengar yoga instructor

'Derek Gladwin's *Rewriting Our Stories* is luminous and declarative about how we can actively shape our stories, and how they shape us. Gladwin writes in spare and lucid prose about how to foster deep and nuanced perceptions that cuts free of fear in order to live meaningfully. A deep love and respect for the transformative power of stories is at the heart of *Rewriting Our Stories*, an exploration about how our imaginations can provoke renewal.'

– Lisa Moore, MFA, professor of creative writing at Memorial University Newfoundland and award-winning author of novels and short story collections such as *February* and *Something for Everyone*

'Derek Gladwin empowers readers to overcome their recurring negative stories, transforming them into empowering narratives. In my work with workplace bullying, harassment and intimidation, I see many fear-filled people with these negative stories. I recommend this book to all of them.'

– Paul Pelletier, LLB, PMP, CAPS, lawyer, workplace consultant, international speaker, and author of *The Workplace Bullying Handbook*

'This book has much to recommend it in terms of originality. It takes the subject of storytelling and embeds it in the wider context. It is not a conventional self-help book; it is a journey through the maze of influencers of the stories that we tell ourselves. It is an exploration of how these stories activate our fears and provides the reader with a clear articulation of these fears. The book stands out as a vehicle to enable people to take back control.'

– Susan Lindsay, PhD, chartered psychologist and director of Montpelier Services, Dublin

FOREWORD

In his new book *Rewriting Our Stories: Education, empowerment and well-being*, Dr Derek Gladwin confirms his reputation as a respected critical thinker, media analyst, narrative coach, and writer in both academic and public forms of scholarship. This makes for a rich, expansive book that invites readers to reconsider *everything* – their emotional status, their personal values, the origin of their belief systems, their culturally acquired behavioural patterns and fears, unconscious social assumptions and practices, and how they want to live their lives.

On the basis that storytelling shapes our existence and influences personal, sociocultural, and public discourses about how we live, Gladwin harnesses the therapeutic power of storytelling to convert feelings of fear and powerlessness into affirmative narratives and efficacious action. He believes that by recognising our recurring negative stories we can rewrite and transform them to achieve greater empowerment and well-being in our lives.

The book begins with the premise that our lives are defined by the 'stories' we live, experience, and tell. Using 'narrative' and 'story' conterminously Gladwin interrogates the multiple contexts in which ingrained negative narratives dominate our thinking and offers suggestions as to how we might identify, confront, and dismantle these oppressive discourses. He suggests that we do so through the process of recognising, reviewing, and rejecting them, then recreating, retelling, reframing, and rewriting our 'problem-saturated' stories until they are functional, positive, and supportive of what we wish to become. This takes time and practice because of how deeply etched such indoctrinated negative narratives can be. However, the steps needed to understand and rewrite them unfold with each chapter of the book, culminating in the seven-stage practice called REWRITE, which provides detailed analysis of the restorying process and instructions on how to achieve it. Additionally, at the end of each chapter readers are invited to pause for personal reflection on what they have read and to decide what resonances the chapter may have evoked for them. In this way the lived reality of the ideas are highlighted.

In *Rewriting Our Stories* Gladwin achieves a balance and blend between abstract reflection and practical direction. He devotes some of the earlier chapters in the book to an extraordinary range of complex philosophical perspectives, while later chapters provide more explicit examples in practical action. In other words, having explored *why* we should rewrite our stories, the book moves into the process of *how* to go about doing this. There are a number of interrelated strands in this book as we progress through the chapters which are separately engaging and collectively fascinating because of the manner in which Derek Gladwin recruits a stunning collection of sagacious thinkers from a vast multidisciplinary and transdisciplinary pool, presenting, integrating, and synthesising their ideas to support and elaborate the belief that at the heart of human health and happiness lies the simple act of storytelling. Storytelling is our antidote to fear.

While recognition of the centrality of narrative in human experience and cultural expression is not new, and while psychology and psychotherapy have long embraced the potential of narrative approaches to therapy, the manner in which Derek Gladwin brings them to public attention is important. It allows us to understand how we can interpret our lives in terms of the stories told to us, the stories told about us, and the stories that we tell ourselves about ourselves. In essence we are hard-wired to tell stories, and the neuropsychological benefits of rejecting unhealthy stories and of narrating our lives positively, appreciatively, with conscious gratitude have wide-reaching health and well-being consequences.

Rewriting Our Stories is not a book to be read quickly or lightly. It is an Aladdin's cave of multicoloured ideas and so it takes concentrated time to absorb and appreciate the diversity of the text. The only way to experience the ideas is to go carefully, page by page, stopping, examining, considering, reflecting, and then undertaking the exercises the author suggests. For example, the book looks at media messages, propaganda, 'misinformation' and 'disinformation', political diktats, religious dogma, discriminatory ideologies, patriarchy and toxic masculinity, the interweave between environmental, social, and economic factors, 'scarcity' narratives, and the social construction of the person. It explores how accumulated messages may make us feel anxious, fearful, deficient, and ineffective because of their unrealistic portrayals of perfection and their inculcation of guilt and shame. Liberation from these 'stories' is offered through intuitive learning, art, creativity, gratitude practice, language, literacy education, imagination, myth, and metaphor in a process that not only empowers us but transforms us as we erase our demeaning internal dialogues that tell us that we are inadequate 'imposters'. Instead Derek Gladwin shows us how to alter these denigratory feelings into positive affirmations of self-worth.

Much space is devoted to the concept of fear, given the times in which we live. The book provides research and statistics in relation to the phenomenal global extent of anxiety and fear:

its specific fight/flight mechanism, its biopsychosocial aspects, and the danger of overreliance on psychopharmacological solutions for culturally ignited problems. While the book does not dwell on the major geopolitical and ideological dangers of our time – threats to democracy, the rise in populism, fascism, totalitarianism, rampant neoliberalism, virological contamination, and ecological instability – these issues form a backdrop to the global culture of fear in which we live. Recognising the role that fear plays in problems of racism, greed, sexism, and violence, the book examines the subjugating personal and cultural messages that we internalise from childhood that repeat themselves like news loops in our heads. These influence our daily behaviour, shape our attitudes, generate prejudices, are ingrained in our perceptions of who and what we are, and impact on our happiness, our health, our hopes, well-being and self-esteem. Again and again Derek Gladwin invites us to 'rewrite' these stories and in this process enrich our lives with self-care, social-care, and empathy for everyone.

Despite Gladwin's cataloguing of toxic belief systems, it would be wrong to imply that this is a book of doom or defeat. It is not. It is impressive how he personalises the book's message, articulates his own particular relationship with the ideas and how he writes poetically, graciously, and gently about the healing process from distress to health. His reference to Yahgulanaas' *Flight of the Hummingbird* (if you do not already know this parable, I am sure you will be moved by it) mirrors his own altruistic disposition in a message to always do *what* you can, *when* you can, *how* you can, to redress whatever needs attention in the world today. This passionate belief in human potential and positive change shines out as the book unfolds. It presents us to ourselves as 'compassionate, caring, and loving beings' who simply want to liberate ourselves from the toxicities that detract from our humanity. Gladwin believes that people are wired for altruism and empathy more than for competition and violence and that they wish to live 'supporting themselves and others, animals and the planet, with purpose and balance for emotional, physical, mental, environmental, and public health'.

In intent, then, this is a book not just for individual benefit but for collective good. It is a text for educators, leaders, psychologists, family therapists, health professionals, journalists, politicians, philosophers, students, youth organisations, and the general public. It repays the time invested in studying it, reflecting on its ideas and enacting the practices it suggests. The overriding message that unites the text is recognition of the vital, precious humanity and potential in each of us, and our capacity to change ourselves and to change the future. This makes it a book for everyone.

Dr Marie Murray, Series Editor, *MindYourSelf*

ACKNOWLEDGEMENTS

All books are collaborative and co-creative efforts. There are the many authors, speakers, artists, filmmakers, and teachers whose outside influences have informed the pages of this book beneath the ideas and experiences on the surface. There are also the people to thank in my life for inspiration, mentorship, and feedback over the years. While it is far too difficult to thank all of the teachers, authors, speakers, friends, colleagues, and family members who have informed this book, it is possible to acknowledge those who directly helped.

I first want to thank those who assisted at varying levels with versions of the book, particularly to those offering editorial support or general feedback: Gretchen Bakke, Mary Chapman, Mark Easby, Wayne Gladwin, Paul Harris, Eva-Lynn Jagoe and Annie Rochette. I am particularly grateful to the editorial wizardry of Gordon Thomas for his insights on earlier drafts.

Next, I want to extend my gratitude to Cork University Press and Atrium (trade imprint) for their belief in the book and support in the production process. The Series Editor for *MindYourSelf*, Dr Marie Murray, provided incredible support and editorial expertise at every stage of the process. Publications Director Mike Collins and Editor Maria O'Donovan steer the CUP ship with precision and poise. Mention must also be made of Alison Burns (Studio 10 Design) and copy editor Aonghus Meaney; I am grateful for the opportunity to work with all of them.

Finally, I am most grateful to Patricia Miranda Barkaskas for all of her love and support over the years this book was conceived and created. She also provided incisive feedback along the way, pushing me in directions that were both uncomfortable and welcomed.

CHAPTER 1

Storytelling in a Time of Fear

We do storytelling

In 2015, the great American novelist Toni Morrison wrote an article titled 'No Place for Self-Pity, No Room for Fear' for *The Nation*'s 150th anniversary issue. In it, she reflects upon a conversation she had with a fellow artist about an increase in violent conflicts around the world, including those perpetuated by her own country.

Morrison expressed how she was struggling to find a reason for joy, or even to write, because of her depression about the global pain and suffering caused by war, poverty, and tragedy. Instead of commiserating with Morrison, the artist friend simply said, 'No, no, no, no! This is precisely the time when artists go to work. That's our job!'

Morrison heeded her friend's advice and concluded her article by writing, 'There is no time for despair, no place for self-pity, no need for silence, no room for fear. We speak, we write, we do language. That is how civilizations heal.' Her closing words serve, in a way, as a guide for this book.

In times of amplified fear and transition, we need art, creativity, and storytelling to help get us through the darker days – to get up and face the world each day, and to resist fear-based responses in our societies and cultures. We also need them to change our paradigms. The processes of creating and experiencing narratives draw us closer to a state of well-being – supporting positive conditions related to health, joy, and stability.

Put simply: we do storytelling. As humans, no matter where our place of origin or when in history, story is at the heart of our societies. We can choose to do storytelling as an antidote to fear. Creating and communicating our personal stories – to ourselves and others – enhances our innate voice and can empower us to engage with one another through empathy and compassion, offering affirmative narratives that bring meaning to our lives.

As Morrison teaches us, our narrative power through the stories we decide to create and tell means we 'must never choose to remain silent, especially in times of dread'. Because we must continually live our stories, we must *do storytelling*. We must *storytell* as an antidote to fear.

Inhabiting our stories

This book begins with the premise that our lives are defined by the stories we live, experience, and tell. We inhabit our stories. Story binds our histories, cultures, and lives together. Story is magical, uncanny, and universally recognised across societies and cultures throughout history. Our stories are the fabric from which we are made and endure: they are *home* and we live in them.

In *The Truth About Stories: A native narrative*, the Cherokee author and professor Thomas King discusses the universality of story in our social histories and in relationship to ourselves. He affirms that the 'truth about stories is that's all we are'. Stories simultaneously define, heal, and create our lives. As King acknowledges, building on long-lasting Indigenous traditions, stories both educate and shape us into who we are in our worlds: 'Stories are wondrous things.'

Drawing on our diverse cultural influences and perspectives, we create stories in our communities. This occurs with each other through multiple versions of ourselves at various nodal points in our lives. Our stories, and the fears and possibilities for hope lodged within them, simultaneously connect us to and separate us from other collective narratives and belief systems.

> *Our stories are home and we live in them.*

Individually, as well as part of the larger collective, we use narratives, images, and metaphors as ways to frame values and desires that ultimately cultivate greater social awareness and create meaning. Storytelling remains a primary way for people to perceive and respond to the world, supporting our own self-care through a process of education and value clarification that helps us reflect on our lives. Much like storytelling, self-care and well-being must also be considered in the context of relationship, to ourselves and to each other simultaneously, rather than only to the Western notion of the 'self' as an isolated and disconnected individual.

Everyone is a storyteller. Recognising our own ability to rewrite our personal narratives allows for creative spaces of personal and social transformation. The real secret to happiness, abundance, success, or whatever states of being people seek in life, lies in the ability to understand and access the abundance of storytelling and the storying process. We use narrative and storytelling to not only understand ourselves, but, perhaps most importantly, appreciate and build relationships with others.

The Anishinaabe author Richard Wagamese observed: 'We're all storytellers, really. That's what we do. That is our power as human beings. Not to tell people how to think and feel and therefore know – but through our stories allow them to discover questions within themselves.' We continue to embark on this process of exploration to discover questions within ourselves, collectively world-building through comparable storytelling, rather than participating in and building a culture of fear.

Empowerment through stories

Based upon the belief that we inhabit our stories and constantly do storytelling, *Rewriting Our Stories* ultimately considers an empowering question: what if we could reduce the power of fear in our lives by simply recognising our recurring negative stories and then rewriting them in ways that serve to enrich our lives? What if this process could improve our physical and mental health, finances, relationships, and overall self-care and well-being? How many of us would examine our own stories to feel more empowered in our lives?

Fear is a primary obstacle to empowerment and well-being, and education about our storying process frees us from much of that fear. Some of the stories we create and tell ourselves produce a heightened state of fear that at best limits our potential to grow in relationships and with ourselves and at worst contributes to depression, anxiety, and disease. By educating ourselves about the influence of stories, we can become more empowered and improve our lives.

It is no secret that the world is currently experiencing high levels of fear, the roots of which go back to conflicts and dynamic cultural shifts during the twentieth century. In *Fear: A cultural history*, the historian Dr Joanna Bourke pinpoints that public policy and our private lives have 'become fear-bound' and that public life is largely administered through the emotion of fear.

Fear has become the primary message produced and reproduced in our society and, as an extension, in our own personal lives – spreading like wildfire throughout our families, communities, and cultures. Fear is part of a larger global pandemic. Perhaps we could go so far as to say that fear is *the* pandemic that causes so many problems of racism, greed, sexism, and violence.

While legitimate fears around our personal and collective safety continue to exist, such as situations of abuse of power, social injustice, illness, or the COVID-19 pandemic (and others similar to it in the future concretely augmenting contamination fear), imagined fears produced through social narratives also proliferate. Many of our stories contain a central theme of fear, which is an enormously powerful force affecting the ways we make decisions and create meaning in our lives. Fear dictates, for instance, how we choose a career, who we vote for, or how we build community.

Fear manifests itself in our personal and collective narratives. Narrative-driven stories are based on real or imagined events that we experience or that naturally weave themselves into the fabric of our lives. The narratives we believe are powerful because they combine our emotions, sensations, experiences, and imaginations synthesised into a dominant story.

An infinitesimal number of stories swirl around us constantly. The problem is that there is always a struggle over who constructs and then controls the dominant narrative, whether it is by mainstream media, politicians, advertisers, families, religion, cultural groups, or even our own minds. Stories are tools that can be harnessed for positive change or used as powerful weapons against ourselves or others. Either we control and narrate our own stories – recreating, retelling, and reframing them – or they will be narrated for us.

Our stories also fit into the larger collective story of our culture, nation, and planet. In *A Way of Being Free*, the Nigerian poet and author Ben Okri talks about how nations and peoples are similarly the stories they feed themselves. He writes: 'If they tell themselves stories that are lies, they will suffer the future consequences of those lies. If they tell themselves stories that face their own truths, they will free their histories for future flowerings.'

Our own stories mirror a similar trajectory, and the pattern of storytelling begins with us. As Okri encourages, we can change our stories from fear to 'future flowerings', opening possibility and opportunity into the narrative. We can see the capacity of our lives to mature in the photosynthesis of sunlight rather than atrophy in oppressive darkness.

Now is the moment for personal and social metamorphosis and to evolve beyond our current culture of fear by reclaiming sustainable stories. Ultimate freedom is a state of managing our fears rather than being controlled by our fictionalised fear stories. 'When we are free from fear', writes the peace activist and educator Satish Kumar, 'we can create conditions conducive to the creativity which is absolutely necessary for human well-being.'

Fear grows through 'problem-saturated' narrative storytelling and influences our beliefs, particularly in how it shapes our ways of knowing and experiencing the world. The result is that we often feel powerless, unmotivated to live fulfilling lives. We sacrifice experience for safety and opportunity for predictability. Does this all sound familiar?

My story is not one of monumental redemption – an epiphany or sudden awakening – as often is the case when one experiences a life-altering event or situation. My story seems more common, though it likely resonates with many others. An insidious but persistent state of fear had subtly, but with accelerated momentum as I grew older, affected my career, relationships, and mental health. Like a virus, fear slowly infiltrated and altered my system over time. I finally realised I needed a remedy.

Upon reflection, one recurring theme became obvious to me: we all design and construct narrative in our lives. I then began to ask myself a series of questions through a narrative-driven lens. How have my stories changed over time? Why are so many of my stories now focused on fear? How do my stories connect to the larger global narrative in sociocultural contexts? In other words, which stories are really about me *alone* or me as part of a *society*? Am I even separate from society?

Because our lives directly influence the various stories we tell ourselves – with some that support us and others that do not – we all have the ability to rewrite our own versions of these narratives each and every day. In this way, we can then begin to address our fears.

Rewriting Our Stories educates us about our collective fear that is both externalised and internalised through narratives. We can empower ourselves to consider alternative narratives and use our new stories about our world to foster well-being in our own lives and, by extension, throughout society.

Transforming how we feel

By following the principles outlined in this book, we will learn *why* we should rewrite our stories from ones dominated by fear to those shaped by the intention of well-being – living to support ourselves, others, animals, and the planet with purpose and balance for emotional, physical, mental, environmental, and public health. Although rewriting stories can produce liberating outcomes in our lives, the main purpose and power of this process is to transform how we *feel* in every moment we live.

Here is the simple premise to move forward with: fear is not an *outcome* but rather a *feeling* in the moment that is largely governed by narrative. The way to minimise fear is to focus on the response in the moment – the story we are generating that perpetuates our fear. Most feelings of foreboding about the future never actually happen. They exist as the stories we tell ourselves that wreak havoc in the moments we construct and accept these as fear-based narratives. In reality, many of our fear narratives are just stories we succumb to when we could be making other choices by writing other stories.

This book explores *why* we should rewrite our stories and then moves into the process of *how* we might go about doing this. By examining the relationships, patterns, and sociocultural networks that contribute to our fear-generated stories, we are invited to enter the unknown or the unexplored depths of ourselves in order to write different stories that are not fear-based.

> When we rewrite our stories, we transform the way we feel each day in every moment.

The aim is to provide an understanding of how we see and process our fears, while offering practical tools to explore our own stories in order to rebuild and rewrite them. The chapters in the book draw on research, knowledge systems, personal experience, and a diverse range of educational guides, including insights from international authors, poets, teachers, leaders, psychologists, therapists, and philosophers, among other experts who offer intercultural perspectives on living and meaning.

The eleven chapters in the book build on specific themes. The first three chapters outline the current culture of fear that we live in, where many social structural systems are rooted in oppression and fear. Chapter 2 focuses on the *why* by considering various patterns that contribute to fear in our lives, detailing some of the foundations of our fear stories. Chapter 3 looks into our social and personal relationship to fear stories through scarcity narratives in culture and the manufactured fear industry.

But this book is only partly about fear. The next four chapters (4–7) serve as a transitionary section that overviews how to overcome patterned stories. This middle part of the book shifts from the *why* to the *how* by outlining some alternative ways of living, perceiving, and experiencing our lives through constructed belief systems, language, opposition, intuition, acceptance, and various forms of intelligence. Chapter 4 teaches us how to locate and then change our paradigm through seeing belief systems as constructed stories, while Chapter 5 guides us through shifting our perspectives and ways of understanding the world. Chapters 6 and 7 provide some tools and approaches to practise changing our paradigms through intuition, acceptance, and surrender.

The early and middle chapters (1–7) serve as a foundation for the remaining four, providing a platform of understanding to educate ourselves about processes within us and what we have learned from our sociocultural systems that led us to initially write our fear stories. Because we live in a culture of fear, in other words, it is no wonder we create and adopt so many fear stories.

The last four chapters (8–11) delve into the influence of narrative storytelling by linking it to our daily lives through language, metaphor, and being present in the moment. Chapters 8 and 9 emphasise living in and then being our stories. The practical application of these ideas is located in Chapter 10, which introduces the seven-stage practice called REWRITE that we can apply to the re-storying process. The concluding Chapter 11 provides guidance on how to practise gratitude in our lives to support the work taken up when exploring and then revisioning fear and other related stories.

Many of us respond to our life circumstances through stories grounded in learned fear-based belief systems, scarcity narratives, or overthinking negative outcomes. In this paradigm, we often base decisions on unknown futures or past experiences, rather than what is actually happening in the present moment and understanding that our responses are largely guided by our narratives and stories.

Living in a sustained fear-induced state creates stress, anxiety, and tension that leads to many physical, emotional, and psychological challenges. It can feel daunting to take the plunge into our fear stories but doing so holds the key to feeling joyful, content, and worthy in our lives.

The vice-grip of fear keeps us from reaching our full potential. The ambition is to arrive at a place where we have the determination and courage to change our lives moment-by-moment and story-by-story. The chapters in *Rewriting Our Stories* serve as different guides to assist in this storying process, and particularly in the context of a contemporary world that contains many challenges if we are to live in a place of well-being.

REFLECTION QUESTIONS

How do you use storytelling in your life on a daily basis? Are you conscious of your connection to storytelling?

When waiting for medical test results, or when facing a job interview or a difficult conversation with a friend, in what ways do you fear the worst rather than envisioning the outcome you actually want?

CHAPTER 2

A Culture of Fear

Everyone experiences fear

Fear is universal. No one can completely escape fear, nor should they. As a fundamental component of evolution, fear alerts us to threats so we can stay safe and remain alive in an unpredictable and precarious existence.

The good news is that we can relate to each other. The bad news is that most of us feel the powerful and debilitating effects of fear too frequently. Dr Brené Brown, the popular researcher on vulnerability and shame, aptly writes in *Daring Greatly*: 'I'd say the one thing we have in common is that we're sick of feeling afraid.' This chapter explores the prevalence of fear in our lives and the impacts fear has on our psyches and health.

Fear is part of our survival as a species within an enormously mysterious and chaotic universe. We all deal with the uncertainty created by the stories we spin about what scares us most. The biggest fear of all is the unknown, or *not knowing*, which manifests in many ways. Serving as perhaps the worst fear we face is the experience of impermanence (often symbolising death). But even just the concept of impermanence, or *not knowing* about *not being*, elicits fear.

Everything we do, even if we attempt to convince ourselves otherwise, is a leap into the unknown. It can be terrifying. To be human and to be alive continuously catapults us into the unfamiliar. That is the moment-by-moment process of *future-making* – or the process of creating, constructing, and producing our personal and social futures. We then create stories about how to cope with our impermanence.

Although seemingly abstract, fear attaches to our experiences and extends into our emotions. In other words, fear is a product of something else. It might feel like it exists on its own, and we are unsure about what we might be afraid of, but it is a reaction to a larger process related to our internal and external experiences. The fear we experience is often perpetuated through oppressive systems of dogma and belief (such as political, religious, or cultural beliefs).

Because fear remains widespread, stories about it proliferate. Stories can be used for understanding and education, as well as for coercion and control. Stories rooted in fear dominate social media, news (mainstream media), family histories, relationships, and politics. Without understanding the concept of fear as socially and culturally constructed stories, it is difficult to see how it penetrates our daily lives and then, by extension, how we can alter and rewrite our stories about it. As a result, a culture of fear should not only be explored, but also questioned and transformed.

Here is where the shift can occur: when we accept that we live in a culture of fear built on stories that are largely fictional. Our mental narratives often tell us we should expect pain and hurt rather than joy, just to be safe and prepared for the worst. This is yet another story, one we have come to believe about our lives in connection with our culture and society through dominant fear stories.

These stories can manifest in various forms throughout mythology, history, religion, philosophy, medicine, psychology, and popular culture. All sorts of narratives attempt to reduce our fears of the unknown, trying to rationalise or mitigate them. Unfortunately, these stories also generate additional layers of fear because they have been conceived by people in systems that are also controlled by fear in many cases.

> *Fear is a reaction to an outcome that cannot be comprehended or rationalised.*

Although it might feel relatively straightforward on the surface, fear is a multifaceted experience. For the purposes of this book, fear will be referred to in a more general sense, even though particular examples and usages might emerge depending upon the context. Because we all experience fear, it is familiar to everyone. As a result, *fear* will be used as a macro or primary emotion and experience. This approach emphasises ways of reducing fear rather than spending too much time categorising and defining the concept of fear itself.

Perhaps the easiest way to begin is by identifying fear as an emotion often brought on by dangers, risks, or threats. The perception of danger is what activates the classic fight-or-flight mechanism, including defence or paralysis. For everyone, fear exists in our evolutionary biology for survival. The problem arises when we function in a state of constant fear even when no real, rather than perceived, risks exist. Living this way has immense consequences in our personal lives, not to mention throughout the networks of society, such as the economy, social institutions, and political governance.

Everyday fear can manifest in many ways. For instance, how many of us can identify with the following questions?

- *Why am I afraid and anxious all the time?*

- *Why does fear control what I do?*

- *Why am I always scared about not being liked?*

- *Why am I paralysed by fear about the safety of my children?*

- *Why do I worry constantly about losing my job and paying my bills?*

- *Why am I scared about feeling so inadequate or feeling like an imposter?*
- *Why do I repeatedly fear being alone?*
- *Why do I feel scared about not having enough or not being good enough?*

Addressing these questions offers a useful starting point. Fear can be a motivating factor to understand what matters to us, how we want to live, and, ultimately, how we create meaning and purpose in our lives. We can use that momentum moving forward.

Fear affects our well-being

The problem with fear is that it can *destroy* as much as *serve* us. Living in a culture of fear can feel oppressive and cause vast numbers of people to suffer unnecessarily. Being in a continual state of fear produces chronic fatigue, depression, anxiety, and other illnesses that all affect our work, motivation, relationships, health, passion, and sexual desire. This state feels like a constant crisis and alters how we experience our lives. There is even a clinical term for this called *catastrophising*, which is the process of regularly imagining the worst outcome when confronted with many possible stories.

The unsustainable effects of fear – which link to stress and anxiety – have become steadily worse. Globally, the number of people who suffer from anxiety is significant. Estimates vary depending on how anxiety is defined, but there is no doubt that anxiety is one of the most pervasive disorders in the global population, given how many people struggle with some form of anxiety at some point during their lifetime.

Mental Health Ireland also confirms the extent to which people experience anxiety-related mental health issues. So, too, across the Atlantic, the National Institute of Mental Health points to the prevalence of anxiety in the adult population.

Apart from the global numbers who suffer with clinical anxiety, there are many people who do not come to clinical attention but nonetheless are besieged by fear and anxiety and suffer serious psychological distress, and the physical effects such distress produces can cause gastrointestinal issues, chronic muscle pain, heart disorders, and cancer, to name but a few.

Research over the past couple of decades confirms our biological relationship to fear, anxiety, and stress. Our bodies physically respond to fear, whether or not the threat is real – whether we are actually running from an attacker or imagining losing our job. Fear induces the body's fight-or-flight mechanism, also known as the stress response, which serves as a necessary warning system to survive external threats.

In *The Fear Cure: Cultivating courage as medicine for the body, mind, and soul*, the *New York Times* best-selling author and founder of the Whole Health Medicine Institute Dr Lissa Rankin explains how our stress response reacts to anything hostile, whether it is a threat to our bodies or an emotional or psychic experience. The fear reaction begins in the amygdala, located in the brain, which is then communicated to the hypothalamus, secreting corticotrophin-releasing factor (CRF) into the nervous system. The CRF triggers the pituitary gland, eventually increasing the stress hormone cortisol.

What comes next is a basic shutdown of all but the most necessary systems in the body, allocating all energy to thwarting the perceived threat initiated by the original fear response. After this process occurs, according to Dr Rankin, our bodies react to fear in the following ways:

- Intestines and colon tense, creating pain and digestion problems, such as diarrhoea, constipation, or nausea.

- Stomach over-produces gastric acid, while digestive enzymes decrease, generating heartburn, acid reflux, ulcers, and other digestive issues.

- Breathing quickens, producing shallow breaths leading to lower oxygen intake and wheezing.

- Heartbeat increases, often creating anxiety attacks with heart palpitations (which feel like minor heart attacks), irregular breathing patterns, and chest pain.

- Body tension increases, particularly in the muscles (shoulders, neck, and jaw), teeth (clenching), and organs, resulting in less oxygen and blood circulation throughout the body.

We have likely all experienced some of these sensations from the stresses of our daily lives. When one or more of them become normalised in the body for long periods of time, chronic illness and disease begin to appear in varying degrees of severity.

The other major biological product of fear is chemical. When our bodies experience fight-or-flight conditions, they produce hormones, including adrenaline and cortisol, to help us survive the danger by functioning at a higher operating state. As Dr Rankin clarifies, cortisol represses the immune system to decrease the inflammatory response that would normally arise from a wound or attack on the body. In this process, our bodies halt routine immunity protection, such as the ability to fight infection or prevent disease, and they marshal all their remaining energy to deal with risks associated with our fears.

Living in a state of fight-or-flight on a daily basis in our modern era has caused immeasurable physical and psychological problems for many people. Why? The simple reason is that our bodies are not built to be in a *constant* fight-or-flight state. It is unsustainable for long durations of time. This process weakens the immune system and opens our bodies up to disease and other health conditions.

Fear and stress in and of themselves are not the problem. Chronic fear, persistent and *constantly recurring* fear, largely based upon fictional stories in our minds, produces stress and tension in the body. The problem arises when we respond to perceived dangers based upon our created fears, rooted in *imaginary* stories.

How many times do we create a fear story about a situation that turns out to be much less severe than our original fear story? How often does that which we fear not happen? Much of what people worry about, outside of real circumstances of abuse, violence, illness, or trauma, for instance, has been manufactured in our culture of fear.

Beyond the pill bottle

Two clear questions arise. Can persistent fear be stopped? If so, how do we stop it? The answer to the first question is *yes*, but it launches us into the second question, one that contains many possible answers.

The common solution to reducing fear and anxiety has been to rely on the pharmacology and psychopharmacology industries. For the portion of the population experiencing severe anxiety, the modern medical solution is usually to prescribe chemicals to stabilise the imbalanced brain chemistry and its neurotransmitters. Over the past ten years, for instance, popular anti-anxiety drugs have been among the leading pharmaceuticals on the market. As a consequence, this overuse has contributed to severe addictions for many people.

Dr Divi Chandna, director of the Center of Mind Body Spirit Medicine in Vancouver, Canada, gave a TEDx talk titled 'The Cure Is Not in the Pill Bottle'. The title sums up our current predicament when addressing rampant conditions such as chronic fatigue, pain and stress, or depression. In fact, one in three people will develop at least one, if not more, of these conditions in their lifetime. They will then turn to the pill bottle to fix them.

Drawing from the American Medical Association, Dr Chandna explains that 80–90 per cent of modern illnesses stem from stress. What is fascinating about such data is that stress places our bodies in a state of constant fight-or-flight response rather than in a condition of balance and relaxation. Because fear creates the stress that leads to most of our illnesses, fear is also a significant factor in contemporary health crises. It debilitates and kills millions of people each year.

As Dr Chandna observes through her clinical and medical work, 'we carry our prisons with us', and our escape to freedom is largely in our control. The cure, and by extension prevention, is in our ability to reduce the fears that create stress in the body. Our emotions ultimately affect our bodies and our health. And yet, most of us have never developed a language or way of explaining our emotional processes to describe accurately how we feel and how to reduce our fears without continued reliance on psychopharmacological solutions.

Fortunately, there is hope. We *can* free ourselves from feeling oppressed by fear. There *are* methods to control and reduce our fears. Rather than viewing our only solution to chronic fear as biochemical and *needing* to be treated with pharmaceuticals, we can also explore the psycho-spiritual elements related to therapeutic storytelling through perception, imagination, and experience.

This book offers alternatives for dealing with a society that functions largely through oppression and fear. Before exploring these methods in later chapters, we will first examine in the next chapter aspects of the greater sociocultural context. How did we get here? How can we change our process?

REFLECTION QUESTIONS

How much of your life is governed by fear? Do you feel oppressed by your fears? Does fear affect your mental health and well-being?

Think of an experience or time in your life when you were mostly healthy, safe, and well. What was governing your life then? What stories were present for you?

CHAPTER 3

Scarcity Narratives

We are enough

This chapter reveals some of the links between scarcity culture and the social stories that have exacerbated our fears, while also considering some alternative sustainable systems of living beyond scarcity. Scarcity, in simple terms, is the gap between what we want and what we can have. It is a fundamental part of a culture of fear, because it represents and embodies a pervasive feeling of lack and deficit and even debt.

Looking at the bigger picture, scarcity culture is based upon the story that tells us *we are never good enough*: *we do not make enough money, we are not beautiful enough, we do not work hard enough*, and *we are not healthy enough*. Do any of these statements of insufficiency sound familiar?

The term scarcity stems from the Old Norman French word *scars* (*c*. 1300), meaning a restriction in quantity. But scarcity has evolved to become a socioeconomic strategy to produce wealth and power. Paradigms built upon and narrated through scarcity are ultimately oppressive and are fundamental to the socioeconomic system in which we all currently function.

In strict economic terms, scarcity results from limited commodities that are in high demand. Creating scarcity – the process of reducing production of a commodity or material goods, such as a vacuum cleaner or a car – manufactures an increased need or desire for that commodity. In other words, the seeming lack of an item or product can justify an artificial or manipulated price increase for profit.

If creating scarcity purposely manufactures competition to generate demand, often of essential goods such as food and water, then how could this strategy produce anything other than fear and anxiety? It assumes that there is only enough pie for some people, so you'd better grab *your* piece now.

Fear generates this type of decision-making. For example, when a resource like fresh drinking water is scarce, if controlled by private interests, the price for bottled water goes up. We saw this with the rise in costs of 'essential goods', such as cleaning agents, hand sanitisers, masks and gloves, at the onset of COVID-19.

Vendors often release concert tickets in batches to give the illusion that there are only a few more tickets to see a popular show, when in fact more tickets remain on hold for later release. This effect induces panic for the consumer/concert-goer, pushing them to buy tickets *now* rather than waiting. Another example is that of oil. Stockpiling barrels of oil has been used as a strategy to increase demand and fetch a higher price per barrel.

Applying the principles of scarcity can increase profits for businesses, but it has also produced an entirely different social outcome: the perpetuation of oppressive attitudes and behaviours. In *Nineteen Eighty-Four*, the haunting novel about fear and control, George Orwell observed that our economic system is a 'deliberate policy to keep even the favoured groups somewhere near the brink of hardship, because a general state of scarcity increases the importance of small privileges and thus magnifies the distinction between one group and another'. The ripple effects of scarcity have been socially harmful. Assisting in creating a culture of fear, scarcity narratives affect people not only economically, but also personally and emotionally.

Looking deeper into the social and cultural effects, the application of scarcity also historically aligns with Western religious theology. The 'Protestant work ethic' purports that *our worth* – literally our salvation and eternal soul – stems from our devotion to work and productivity. The thinking goes like this: our labour serves as *good works* contributing to our worth and salvation. The framework of the Anglo-European, British, and North American cultural tapestry contains these historical threads, and they remain entrenched in society even today, regardless of if we identify as being Protestant or not.

Similar to the Protestant work ethic framed as a cultural phenomenon, the system of capitalism insists that work and productivity lead to pleasure and satisfaction because, as the story goes, it allegedly breeds autonomy and freedom. Capitalism has been aligned with the story of freedom for a couple of centuries, even though it often limits our freedoms and traps us in a life of debt, scarcity, and overwork in the pursuit of never-ending growth and wealth production. Time off exists only to prepare for more productive work.

In the current mode of capitalism called *neoliberalism*, enough is *never* enough; we must always work and be productive to sustain economic growth. Never-ending growth remains the constant. But, as we know, endless growth by definition is impossible.

Scarcity underlines the basic philosophy of this socio-economic system that governs every aspect of our lives, creating desperate people who are workers motivated by fear and, as a consequence, distracted as citizens. How can we question systems of power that oppress us when we are too busy working? That is the point!

The German sociologist and political economist Max Weber famously considered these connections at the beginning of the twentieth century in his book *The Protestant Ethic and the Spirit of Capitalism*. As Weber points out, within the capitalist system it is not *enough* to work and sustain yourself; rather, one must do *more than enough* to gain wealth and prosperity.

Success and happiness exist as prescribed narratives to work harder and increase wealth. This is defined as the 'spirit of capitalism', according to Weber. Embedded in this phrase, we see the unlikely marriage between economics and salvation theology, between capitalism and Protestant ethics.

Why is this relevant now? Why should we spend time on seemingly abstract economic history? Scarcity is a story of fear deeply entrenched in our cultural psyche with historic roots in capitalism and religion. Those promoting capitalism found an unlikely ally in Christian theology, even though the teachings and practices of Jesus do not reflect such alignment.

Within a model of scarcity, we have also been acclimatised to worship wealth and power because they are, according to the story, motivating us to work precisely because of the myth that if we do so, we too can become wealthy. Working hard can be a cathartic experience. The problem lies in the process by which work aligns with our worth and, even more so, our destiny or salvation.

A culture of scarcity perpetuated by religious and economic belief systems is designed to produce a working population, one that will either be too tired to participate in the social process to promote change or literally work themselves to death in order to maximise profits for companies.

The reason for identifying the root cause of scarcity narratives in the Western world is to underline how much it affects our current culture and society by increasing fear and anxiety. By definition, scarcity decrees that there is never enough to satisfy us, and we must make trade-offs to acquire what we want and need. By feeling we do not *have enough*, which leads to feeling we *are not enough* as people, we are then driven further to produce more and work harder. This cycle never ends.

HORATIO ALGER MYTH

The late-nineteenth-century tale of 'rags to riches' relied on the belief that the hardest worker with good morals becomes the richest and most successful person. Like many popular narratives rooted in culture, it came primarily from two novels by Horatio Alger during the Gilded Age: *Ragged Dick* (1868) and *Brave and Bold* (1872). The similar story on which the novels are based, known as the 'Horatio Alger Myth' or more popularly now as the 'American Dream', remains one of the most trotted-out fictional narratives in Western culture.

The Alger Myth is one significant reason why many people with low incomes support political stories of the ultra-wealthy. They believe the story that it is *good for the economy* to lower tax rates for the top 1 per cent of the wealthiest people rather than supplying more liveable resources (i.e., housing, food, or medical subsidies) and tax relief for everyone else. In this story, people believe that someday they might become a billionaire, part of the 1 per cent, embracing this concept even if it negatively affects their lives in the present. Rooted in scarcity and fear, this story exists specifically to convince populations to sustain policies and elect people to power that do not support their own interests. It is an historical story, one that author John Steinbeck commented on back in the mid-twentieth century: the poor in America cannot see themselves as exploited, but instead as 'temporarily embarrassed millionaires'.

It is a loop we remain trapped in without an apparent escape.

Let us now look at some of the common stories of scarcity both within and separate from the socioeconomic models discussed above. Can we identify with any of these questions?

- *Is my identity aligned with my job?*
- *Do I feel like a failure or an impostor in my life?*
- *If I take a day off work, do I feel guilty or ashamed?*
- *Do I feel unworthy if I don't have enough social media followers?*
- *Do I believe that I am doing enough to change the world?*
- *Do I see myself as an adequate parent or do I think I have failed my children?*
- *Do I constantly worry about money?*
- *Do I see myself or do other people see me as attractive?*

I am sure everyone can relate to some of these questions. We write these stories about our own lives, and often to the detriment of our personal and social well-being. We can use storytelling generatively, to help create equality, opportunity, and possibility, by rewriting the deceptions of scarcity that currently exist within a culture of fear.

Living by and believing in these deceptive stories produces and reproduces a culture of fear. Only through our fear of scarcity might we be motivated to work harder, buy more beauty products, and yet feel more inadequate regardless of what we purchase, which continues the destructive cycle all over again. Sound familiar?

Acknowledging scarcity, and the power it has over our lives, is revelatory and transformative. It is vital for all of us to recognise that the pervasive narrative of scarcity is a fabrication. It stamps 'deficiency' on us from the second we are born to the moment we die.

Addiction and trauma author Dr Gabor Maté writes: 'No human being is empty or deficient at the core, but many live as if they were and experience themselves primarily that way.' Scarcity stories flow through the veins of society and culture, leaving us all feeling inadequate and fearful. It is no wonder we seek so many empty ways to fill the gap of deficiency rather than accept at the outset that *we are already enough*.

The fear industry

One of the major challenges to transforming our social paradigms is that fear stories *sell*. How many of us love consuming news? Whether it involves debates, pundits, conversations, or interviews, it is compelling to watch the ways people attempt to tell/sell their stories to promote potential change. Sometimes the stories align and sometimes they differ, but they all encapsulate personal and collective perspectives.

Despite enjoying the narrative aspect of news, the experience often leaves us anxious or depressed because news stories are usually about fear in some form or another. Crisis has become our daily story. Truth and credibility have taken a backseat to sensationalism and fear. When people do not have their own stories to tell, they often adopt the dominant stories of crisis and fear as their own.

Genuine crises, such as natural disasters, accidents, or even death, have occurred all over the planet since the beginning of existence. But crises are intensified by how they are reported –

or narrated as stories – and this happens more often when they are manufactured for consumption, profit, and entertainment. The 24-hour news cycle perpetuates this problem.

> *Storytelling has become a business of fear, where selling is more valuable than telling.*

For many people, breaking news reports about other people's distress are far more compelling to watch than news about peace and prosperity. If we are appalled by the suffering during these crises, then why are we, as a society, captivated by these stories?

People have become largely acclimatised to the drama of fear narratives. Good news is never as exciting as something outrageous or violent that mirrors and normalises our own feelings of fright and terror.

Part of the success of global populist movements comes from sensationalism produced by chronic crisis and fear. Populism historically goes through waves of popularity. It emerges out of a desire by certain groups of people, who believe their voices are ignored, to feel more power in the political and social process.

Often rooted in historic forms of oppression or dogma, such as religious, nationalist, or discriminatory ideologies, populist narratives are largely fear-based and reactionary. This is why they are usually short lived and go through waves. They draw on a subjective *enemy* or *other* in a zero-sum game with a clear winner and loser (also see Chapter 5). In this context, scapegoating the *other* provides people with a sense of injustice and purpose to support self-serving positions.

One example of this pattern is the resurgence of propaganda stories, now so-called 'fake news', where any entity can pose as a credible source for news, despite the lack of veracity or evidence. Of course, those who wish to discredit authentic news can equally level the claim that it is fake, a strategy beloved by populists. By doing so, we are left in a vortex in which the credibility and veracity of anything we are told is suspect.

Truth in this model is based upon who rewrites the story. The concept of 'fake news' – more accurately called *misinformation* and *disinformation*, where audiences are either accidentally or purposely deceived – has a long history. Lies and deception in the news are, at their core, forms of propaganda designed to influence masses of people to bolster political, religious, or financial groups.

Another example uses the power of storytelling as a type of branding in the collective narrative. In *Storytelling: Bewitching the Modern Mind*, the writer and researcher Christian Salmon outlines how narrative has been explicitly used as an instrument of corporate and political control since the mid-1990s.

What he identifies as 'the narrativist turn' is a shift from previous methods of using logos and branding to exploit consumers and citizens in the 1980s. Story provides more effect because of the ways it resonates so deeply in the DNA of humanity. Because of this turn, Salmon argues, 'storytelling has been able to emerge as a technology of communications, control, and power'.

Even storytelling can be co-opted to obtain or retain power. The term 'storytelling management', according to Salmon, refers to when companies, news organisations, or political candidates use storytelling as a control agent to generate fear.

Collective forms of storytelling persist throughout history. But using storytelling as formal corporate management styles exercises the power of story to exploit and coerce both employees and consumers (referred to as *audiences*) in order to sell a product, idea, or emotion.

Examples of storytelling management exist everywhere. Consider how advertisers no longer sell a brand or product but a story. It could be a family buying a new car, a couple experiencing a new restaurant, or a group of women enjoying a night out in a wine bar wearing a specific brand of clothing. The product is now subordinate to the story.

The narrativist turn is more than simply selling a product. It also sells fear. Fear is not only a control agent, but, as we see with scarcity socioeconomics, also a money-maker. In times of uncertainty, fear mobilises people to support politicians, movements, or initiatives outside of their own interests, whether it is part of the narrativist turn or disinformation campaigns. This is why ratings of political leaders rise in times of crisis. Fear begets more fear, creating an endless cycle of fear.

Building a sustainable global story

Looking at patterns of fear in the sociocultural context of scarcity and the crisis industry also informs us of possible futures. How might we build sustainable narratives moving forward? How do fear stories impede such progress?

The theory of sustainability considers how people, economies, animals, and the Earth, for example, rely upon each other. They are interdependent. Sustainability ultimately asks: what if, as the starting point, we make decisions with everyone's health and well-being in mind, particularly those living on other parts of the planet? The health of our personal lives extends from the condition of our social and physical environments.

Sustainability also serves as a social term, both connected to but also separate from explicit ecological circumstances (see Figure 1). Democratic societies must work together for the collective good. Looking at the most basic example, the relationship we have with our neighbours could alter the way we live on a daily basis. Cultivating those relationships matters because they directly influence our lives and the equanimity of a community.

Figure 1: Sustainability diagram indicating the interwoven relationship between the environmental, social, and economic factors, with environment and society serving as the foundation.

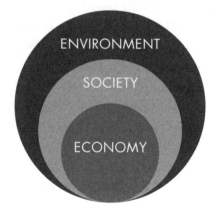

Fear, however, impedes cooperation. Pervasive fear paralyses and stagnates rather than sustains. Our environments – including but not limited to neighbourhoods, communities, families, and governments – can only survive as long as the social collective finds concord through interconnection (see Figure 2). Fear dismantles connection and remains unsustainable for both the greater social sphere and for individuals.

Figure 2: Social sustainability of well-being

Social sustainability can affect our personal fear stories. Politics may often seem like an esoteric practice relegated to a collective few who appear to care primarily about power and greed. But the political process – and those who serve within it – can lead to serious consequences for everyone. Elected officials and the laws they uphold or challenge can have severe effects, not just in the specific countries in which they legislate, but also around the entire planet. Democracies are only successful if all citizens participate in the process. As the saying goes, *elections matter*.

Political systems, like everything else related to human history, rely upon stories. We construct stories about our societies and the *best* system to uphold them. Successful politicians, regardless of how well they serve their constituents, understand how to tell stories. They rely on stories to be elected and re-elected.

The journalist and author George Monbiot discusses in his book *Out of the Wreckage: A new politics for an age of crisis* how global politics is searching for a new story, which hopefully 'is positive and propositional rather than reactive and oppositional'. Telling the 'right story' and learning 'how to tell it' infiltrates and influences everyone across the political spectrum. Monbiot acknowledges that the people who tell and control stories run the world.

Building on Monbiot's observation, the world needs new social and political stories as much as people need to rewrite their personal stories. Those who can rewrite their stories can govern their own lives without so much pain and suffering. There is recursivity between personal and societal stories. Our stories ripple outwardly into the social realm.

As the feminist movement has demonstrated for centuries, the personal *is* the political. There is so much wisdom in this statement. How can we create stories that serve rather than destroy us, ones that engage our own self-care needs as well as those of our social worlds? Self-care must also be considered as a form of relationship-building with ourselves and others.

The Western world has, yet again, a lot to learn from the teachings of Indigenous societies. Along with the knowledge and values within them, these paradigms of abundance and equity emphasise sustainable relationships with both the human and the non-human world as a foundational way of living. Knowledge transmission and memory move through story and restorying. Everything and everyone are in relationship with each other. Deficit-based scarcity thinking cannot function in this paradigm. The personal *is* the global.

The purpose of this chapter was to understand how and why fear remains integral to our daily lives and how fear ties to fundamental aspects of culture and society, particularly through collective social stories of scarcity, crisis, and political narratives. As the next chapter will explore, we all have opportunities to free ourselves from oppressive fear stories by overcoming the patterns that underpin them.

REFLECTION QUESTIONS

How does scarcity function in your life? Do you ever feel you are not enough or that what you do in the world is never enough?

Can you think of any fears you may be feeling in this moment? How many of these fears are based upon external social stories related to scarcity, crises, or political narratives?

CHAPTER 4

Seeing Belief Systems as Stories

Oppressive belief systems

A culture of fear and its social and personal consequences, as explained in the previous chapters, relies upon constructed and reinforced belief systems which are responsible for how we initially 'write' many of our own stories. The following four chapters will broadly address the issue of overcoming patterned stories *built upon pervasive belief systems* in our lives.

We will begin this chapter by examining some oppressive belief systems – what they are and how they develop. We all live by belief systems, whether or not we are conscious of them. Unfortunately, we are not often aware of their hold over us. Belief systems govern our values and ways of perceiving the world, which affect so many of our choices and experiences. They influence our relationships, affect our health, and dictate how we function in every moment.

Both personally and socially we can construct our worlds as much as our worlds might construct us. *Social constructionism* is a way of explaining how our beliefs about the world depend upon how we approach, interpret, and learn about our constructed reality through relationships (including with our 'self'). Put another way, we are *socialised* or influenced to value certain beliefs and behaviours, or stories, over others, based on our sphere of social conventions.

The fundamental premise of social constructionism is that knowledge systems and the world around us are not *real* or absolute in themselves. This is why we can use a subjective term like *beliefs* and consider them in a *systemic* way that is structural and deeply engrained in society. What is *real* to us is entirely dependent upon our constructed context.

Our *identity*, for example, might shift in various groups or contexts – how we react in situations or how others react to us. Identity is based upon our relationships as much as the constructed idea of the 'self'. Our identity, then, is a mutable story contingent upon who is creating it at any moment.

Because our beliefs are constructed value systems, they are inherited and learned within a fixed social system. They have been assembled by society – through families, education, law, religion, the state, or pop culture – and have surrounded us since we were children. Some of these constructed beliefs are beneficial, such as the idea of family that serves as a unit of support and education, but many can be damaging because they themselves have been constructed out of fear.

Fortunately, we can construct new belief systems at any point in our lives (see Figure 3). We can imagine our constructed worlds as stories that can be rewritten.

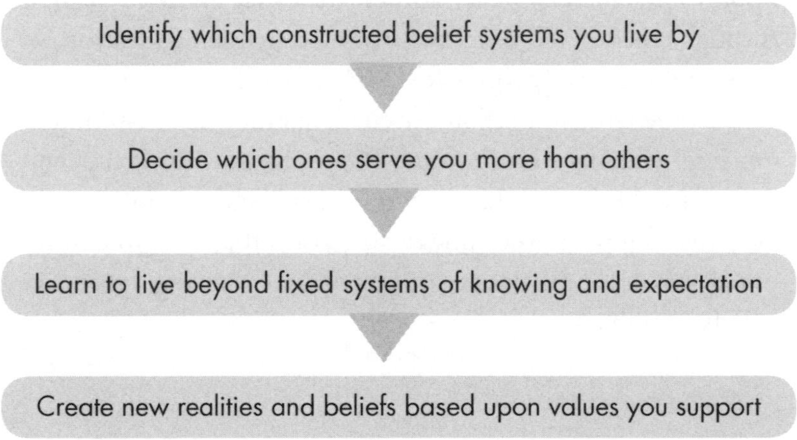

Identify which constructed belief systems you live by

Decide which ones serve you more than others

Learn to live beyond fixed systems of knowing and expectation

Create new realities and beliefs based upon values you support

Figure 3: How to shift your belief systems

The English poet and painter William Blake recognised over two hundred years ago, 'I must create my own system or be enslaved by another'. These lines from the fallen angel Los in Blake's book *Jerusalem* are followed by: 'I will not reason and compare: my business is to create.' The poetic metaphor here is apt for understanding our own social construction: we are in the business of creating stories rather than blindly inheriting others. It also provides an important link between systems and creation in the form of stories and storytelling.

While seemingly simple to understand, the practice of unlearning and rewriting our belief systems can prove challenging because of the ways in which they have influenced our ideas, perceptions, and relationships. Belief systems are often riven with fears that are based on falsely perceived truths, and oftentimes even outright fictions.

Many of the ways we have been socialised to privilege certain ideas over others have emerged from systems built upon oppression. These systems also create social division, such as through constructed differences of race, gender, education, or class, and ultimately foster fear and control.

Such beliefs can pose many challenges for us, including in our interpersonal relationships. The problem with such pervasive cultural beliefs is that they serve no one's best interests. In fact, they support other power structures that seek to control or oppress us. For instance, are any of the following oppressive beliefs relatable?

I am inadequate.

Women should always be nice and smile.

Men cannot fail.

Vulnerability is a sign of weakness.

My job is who I am.

My children's behaviour is a direct reflection upon me.

I am never good enough.

Everyone is out to get me.

Because I was abused as a child, I will always be broken and unlovable.

Other people know what is good for me more than I do.

It is my responsibility to fix everyone else's problems.

Let us consider a historically significant source of our oppressive belief systems: patriarchy. We could look at many dominant belief systems as an illustration, but patriarchy has spawned so many other oppressive belief systems it is worth discussing as one of the primary sources still widespread in our lives today.

Patriarchy was originally defined as a system where men held all of the power, largely through privileged positions received via lineage inheritance. Family wealth, for instance, is often inherited through generations of sons. Within this constructed system, men retain their power by holding social, political, economic, and judicial leadership and influencing dominant belief systems. As a consequence, power begets power and the cycle continues.

Much like the Horatio Alger Myth of the American Dream discussed in the previous chapter, the *self-made man* is a constructed story. Everyone's succession to power comes through relationships of some kind, whether they are equitable or part of a rigged system. We are all interconnected and co-create with each other. Perhaps the phrase *socially constructed man* is more accurate because patriarchy remains protected and perpetuated by ongoing belief systems of those holding power and those reinforcing that narrative.

If there is any doubt about the continual influence of patriarchy in contemporary society, one only has to look at the fact that a small number of men currently own 90 per cent of the world's wealth, while women across the globe perform two-thirds of the labour, which is almost always underpaid and, in many cases, unpaid.

What is important to recognise here is that the effects of patriarchy extend well beyond systems where only men hold power. This dominant belief system has hatched value systems of competition, hierarchy, abuse, violence, slavery, exploitation, and oppression upon which many laws are based. While contemporary manifestations are often expressed through male power, and linked to misogyny and wealth production, patriarchy is a system of oppression and the values it upholds may be found in any person who consciously or unconsciously upholds those values.

These value systems also contribute to forms of damaging *toxic masculinity*, affecting young children, their gender and sexual identities, their professional aspirations and relationships, and their perceptions of themselves as they grow into adulthood. People often unknowingly support patriarchy because this belief system still drives much of society and burdens everyone in the process.

> *The social effects of patriarchy, and the belief systems growing out of it, continually infiltrate our personal and social stories.*

The prevalence of oppressive belief systems, such as economic and gender inequality, or religious, racial, and cultural supremacy, as well as patriarchy, means that it can be extremely challenging to separate what is best for us from those who want to control us for profit or power. Belief systems result from socialised and constructed behaviour imposed upon us as *normal* or the *status quo* by people who fear any social or cultural transformation that may negatively impact them.

Belief systems framed as social narratives are some of the most potent generators of fear because of the magnitude of their power. The historical interpretation of Judeo-Christianity, for example, insists we are all born flawed. The concept of *original sin* holds that all people have been tainted by sin and therefore need saving by God to find salvation in this life and the afterlife.

The result of this dominant Western belief system – whether one accepts it as their truth or not – is that, from our earliest cognitive awareness, we learn to feel shame for being flawed or tainted as a *sinner*. This story creates personal blame for all of humanity's mistakes. The irony here is that the teachings of Jesus did not promote beliefs of fear, but those of love, compassion, and acceptance. Interestingly, the term 'communism' comes from Christianity through the Catholic Church, according to the philosopher Jean-Luc Nancy, where a 'communist good' is something that belonged to the community, not a single person. But belief systems are often perpetuated by those who have vested interests in oppression over others to establish and maintain power rather than those who are invested in building community and democratic society.

The ideology and socioeconomic system of capitalism discussed in Chapter 3 stems partly from patriarchy, as does colonialism. In combination, these three historically ubiquitous belief systems – the fear triad of *capitalism, patriarchy, and colonialism* – teach society that people are served best when in competition with and separated from one another.

In these three systems, individualism and fractured society, rather than collectivity and relationality, are prized above all else because individuals can be easily oppressed through fear more than by communities supporting one another in the democratic process of difference. Elements of the triad – which are used throughout this book as illustrative examples because of their power, omnipresence, and impact over our lives – promote convincing stories and attitudes that breed fear.

We often think that the *other person* must be *out to get us* and, in turn, we believe we need to be out to get the other person. What causes people to behave in this way are personal and societal stories steeped in fear, scarcity, and oppression. These social narratives that produce disharmony seep inward and come to dominate our personal stories. Sometimes these divisive narratives result in extremist movements or hate groups with displaced rage towards others. Regardless of the stories devised to divide us, too many of which remain to this day, people are wired for altruism and empathy more than for competition and violence.

Exposure to other stories

A key point so far in this chapter is that people are not born with their belief systems. They are socially constructed and learned over time. We are taught what to believe about ourselves, others, and the world through our families, cultures, and societies.

Depending upon the pedagogical model, education can play a significant part in helping us to learn or unlearn these narratives. As a start, perhaps everyone could adopt this affirmative story: *I am not the belief systems I have learned.* Or, even better: *I am the character in the story I want to write.*

One pedagogical model provides a useful way of seeing the various elements active in our own developing stories. It is called CEE: Culture, Education, and Experience. Every person understands the world through beliefs learned through the building blocks of CEE.

We often do not see that CEE patterns are unique to each person in how they view the world. Or, we can forget that a person's belief systems remain fundamental to their behaviours. When this happens, we often criticise another person for saying something offensive or for doing something in public that seems rude, such as jumping the queue or not greeting us. We might feel hurt and then blame another person for what feels invasive.

We become *outraged* by what is misunderstood CEE. Such misguided outrage is often the result of underestimating our capacity or desire to acknowledge another person's culture, their educational opportunities, or their life experiences, if they differ from ours.

Our perception of another person or their culture is dependent upon our expectations, and we can be unaware of our ignorance of their lived experiences and their personal culture, education, and experience. Learning that each person views their own version of the world through their CEE path and that a person's belief systems remain fundamental to their socialisation can be one of the best forms of education.

For instance, some cultures believe queuing in line for events or in public spaces is a *proper* or *civil* way to wait, while other cultures do not hold these cultural beliefs. Growing up in North America, and particularly on the west coast, I was educated in my culture to always stand politely in line or let a vehicle have the right of way when pulling into traffic.

When I travelled to China and India as a young adult, the situation was vastly different. Queuing is not an observed cultural practice. If one is not familiar with this difference, public spaces can feel like utter chaos.

I remember patiently queuing in a long line for a popular restaurant in Darjeeling, India. The line did not seem to be moving. I finally noticed many people cutting in front of me up at the front of the line. *What is this about*, I grumbled to myself. *How rude! This is unbelievable*. Regardless of feeling a sense of what I *thought* was justified outrage, I said nothing and let my anger fester and build.

> *Assumptions are the little cracks in the deteriorating footpath of expectation.*

After a few days of this exasperating experience, it finally dawned on me that the practice around queuing is not the same in my culture. In one instance, a person cut in front of me while giving me a warm smile. *There's no malice*, I thought to myself. *This must be just part of the culture. There's no other explanation.* After this vital insight about distinctive values around waiting in line, I eventually assimilated into the culture and pushed my way through like everyone else.

Despite my discomfort with this practice, I watched those who I observed to be experts in order to adopt the 'best practices' of getting through the queue quickly. Women in their eighties were some of the most ruthless and adept people at finding their way through long queues. To my amazement, they would always find a way to the front. Elbows and hips would be used efficiently in manoeuvring their way through throngs of people. Needless to say, I quickly learned to follow in the wake of these women – both literally and metaphorically!

Once I returned to North America, and later when living for short periods of time in Ireland and the UK, where orderly queuing is observed, I had a newfound respect for people from other cultures who did not follow the queuing etiquette. *They are not being offensive or discourteous. They just have a different set of values and beliefs than my own.*

Unless challenged, we see much of the world through our own socially constructed CEE-tinted glasses. This is partly why it is important to regularly expose ourselves to other stories, cultures and experiences. Understanding both our own *and* other people's way of perceiving our surroundings remains an essential practice if we are to cultivate compassion and empathy. It is also vital for reading our own stories written over a lifetime and then deciding which of those stories that are embedded in our belief systems we want to rewrite.

Shattering the illusion

As another illustration, let us turn to a literary example to show links between our personally held stories and overcoming our belief systems. Hermann Hesse was a German-Swiss Nobel-prize-winning author known for his spiritually motivated novels in the early to mid-twentieth century. Hesse's novel *Siddhartha*, for instance, famously discusses the process of shattering through our learned belief systems to understand the infinitesimal and interchangeable number of other beliefs available to us. The novel captures the process of questioning how we know what we know or value what we do.

This process is both liberating and frightening. With the possibility of freedom comes fear of uncertainty and impermanence, leading to a universal conundrum: we cannot have freedom without the possibility of fear. We can, however, experience freedom without fear dominating it.

In one of his semi-autobiographical novels titled *Demian*, Hesse writes about his own process of self-realisation, one that explores the association between the real world, what he calls a world of 'illusion', and the spiritual or mystical world. This initiatory process of exploration, which begins at a young age for the protagonist Emil Sinclair, examines different and often contrasting belief systems: ones he grew up believing in his middle-class German-Swiss family before the First World War and others he develops later along with his classmate and mentor Max Demian.

Fear serves as a shadow permeating this novel because, Hesse wrote it during the First World War and published it in 1919. The book asks how might a person growing up amidst such fear and uncertainty seek to examine their own identity?

How might one person's story connect to a larger collective story surrounded by fear and instability? Can belief systems change in a context of such upheaval?

The answers return us to Toni Morrison's advice at the start of this book: 'There is no time for despair …. We speak, we write, we do language. That is how civilizations heal.' In other words, we write our stories; that is how we heal and grow.

Our stories define us. But these definitions remain changeable, depending upon a person's ability to revise or rewrite old stories that continue to frame that person. Understanding how these systems of being in the world – linked to our CEE – can generate change and growth in a quest for empowerment and well-being.

Stories of love

Our lives intertwine with our patterned stories, which are often inflexible and entrenched beliefs we rarely question or attempt to change. Storytelling remains the unifying element of all human experience. The difficulty arises when our stories are influenced by exclusionary and discriminatory beliefs rooted in fear.

Regardless of the challenging systems in which most of us are entrenched – whether colonial paradigms of hierarchy, socioeconomic systems of capitalism based upon greed and competition, or the dominant power structures of patriarchy – these systems are only maintained through ongoing beliefs and archetypal stories perpetuated on a mass level.

When many of our beliefs arise from dominating systems of oppression, we cannot live meaningfully or supportively with ourselves or others. This produces a state of disharmony because we are out of balance.

In *The Four Agreements: A Toltec wisdom book*, Don Miguel Ruiz discusses how 95 per cent of our belief systems are largely fictional until we wake up and see another story. He suggests that much of our suffering comes from the extent to which we believe the 'lies' we are programmed to believe from birth. These are not designed for our well-being.

Such narratives can be changed and replaced with generative stories about collective and personal support for one another. We are all, at our core, compassionate, caring, and loving beings. When we do harm to others or ourselves, it is often because we just want to be loved but find ourselves controlled by toxic beliefs. Understanding the patterns and relationships of social belief systems fundamentally alters how we first recognise and then rewrite our own stories.

> *Everyone wants to be loved, but sometimes we find ourselves in the wrong story.*

The world is overflowing with love, despite what we perceive to be happening around the planet. Love drives people's most meaningful stories. Love motivates action, while fear generates apathy.

When people are in genuine crises, it is not usually corporations or institutions that perform heroic acts of support. It is the people – family members, neighbours, friends, teachers, and even strangers – who support, protect, and love one another. During crises we hear numerous stories about people rising up beyond their own self-interests to help one another, putting themselves in danger to help those in need. If we overcome destructive belief systems in times of crisis, then how might we do the same in our everyday lives? This is a significant question for our current times of environmental, mental, public health, and social uncertainty.

The good news is that our beliefs can be reconstructed and transformed. The values influenced by our beliefs are not imprinted upon us permanently. People can choose different values and create new stories that reflect beliefs that support their development and purpose in life. As the next chapter will show, altering belief systems also relies upon shifting our paradigms and the language and thinking that go along with them.

REFLECTION QUESTIONS

What are some of your learned or constructed belief systems? Do they align or misalign with what you value?

What fears arise when exploring or even challenging your inherited belief systems? Can you imagine an alternative story based upon a different set of beliefs and values about your life?

CHAPTER 5

Shifting the Paradigm

Conscious perception

One of the underlying principles of this book is how we might alter the way we consciously perceive the world. Such a process, which is the focus of this chapter, involves being fully present to ourselves, our relationships, and to the world around us.

We achieve such *conscious perception* not only through understanding our systemic stories, as outlined in the previous chapter, but also in reclaiming and constructing authentic stories that align with more meaningful and empowering beliefs in our lives. Put another way: we can rewrite our stories by unlearning older narratives and teaching ourselves how to create new ones. This seemingly simple practice underscores our existence and has the power to transform our lives and those of the people around us.

The ability to view the world through other forms of perception outside of the rational mind largely develops out of the capacity to cultivate the actions of listening, feeling, and trusting, rather than through reaction, anxiety, hate, and distrust. Thinking without drawing on deeper modes of perception leads to many of our problems. Not to overstate it, but perception is everything.

Perception defines our reality, providing interpretation, identification, and organisation that alters the fundamental ways we experience the world and act in it. Such experiences rely not only on personally inherited stories, explains Dr Jeffrey J. Kripal in *The Flip: Epiphanies of mind and the future of knowledge*, but also the many stories that provide different ways of creating forms of reality. Much of our perception of what we might call *reality* depends upon the stories we live by.

Because the research on perception and cognitive science is vast and much too large to address here, for the purposes of this book perception will be framed as a way of knowing, seeing, and experiencing that also involves recognising the fear-based narratives that we have learned throughout our lives and, as humans, throughout history. The capacity to perceive consciously is essential to reviewing perspectives that undermine societal potential.

> *One of the major crises we experience is one of perception.*

William Blake explored perception a great deal, particularly in his revolutionary book of poems, prose, and illustrations titled *The Marriage of Heaven and Hell*. Blake was a mystical and social justice poet (to use a contemporary expression) as much as he was an originator of the Romantic poetic tradition in British literature from 1790 to 1830.

The Romantic movement was, in part, a response to increased industrialisation and economic policies that mechanised humans and exploited what were (and still are) considered *natural* resources (including human labour). Confronting such dehumanising practices, Blake, along with some other Romantic poets, sought to reframe how we might experience the world by recreating the systems that guide our existence. Their purpose – of considering other ways of knowing and experiencing outside of rational Enlightenment thinking – remains with us today.

Of note, *The Marriage* was also created between 1790 and 1793 during the time of the French Revolution. Transformation was in the air, and poets and authors as storytellers generally provide a deep understanding of current and alternative paradigms.

Framed as a conversation between Heaven and Hell, Blake challenges the perceived duality between good/bad or right/wrong by demonstrating how they interact. More directly, Blake unifies the polarities to show interconnectedness. A good portion of Blake's book is spent in Hell, which functions as another plausible perspective and not necessarily representing the opposite of Heaven. Life is much more diverse and multi-dimensional than simple opposition.

Blake reminds us powerfully and beautifully that if 'the doors of perception were cleansed', we would be able to lift ourselves beyond the narrow 'chinks' of our limited earthly perceptions and infinitely expand our comprehension. In doing so, he identifies how we only perceive reality selectively. The word 'cleansed' serves as a metaphor for clarity and indicates a blockage of our own doing that when cleared opens our ability to consciously perceive and shift limiting paradigms into more expansive ones.

Blake's insights anticipate the discriminatory viewing of news and social interaction in contemporary culture. Because of our insulated social circles, we increasingly base our perception on the social media platforms we belong to and the algorithm-based internet silos that can limit our social interaction, whether they connect to friends, work, church, or family.

In these online worlds, people are less obliged to interact with those whose thoughts and values differ from their own. This can entrench further their belief systems as the only forms of reality because they are not challenged enough by people with alternative views.

This process ultimately creates a *confirmation bias* – or the practice of constantly researching, interpreting, or acquiring knowledge that only affirms our own limited beliefs. The 'doors of perception' are constructed through the socialising process of our prescribed cultural belief systems – now through saturated media consumption that is riven with what some deride as 'fake news' instead of what is perceived as impartial, unbiased reporting. The result often leads to further division and cynicism rather than understanding and connection to each other. Confirmation bias delegitimises the notion that we are wired for human interconnection more than fear and oppression.

The key to opening the doors of perception is through narr-ative, spawning awareness through relationship, and particu-larly our ability to 'cleanse' or recreate the stories from systems of fear to those of connection and plurality. We can experi-ence limitless opportunity when our stories become 'infinite', as Blake expresses it. Narratives are endless and consistently renewing.

Overcoming opposition

To be human is to write stories in union with the billions of other people writing their stories simultaneously. We can all attain awareness through using conscious perception to widen the doors of the infinite, which is to say into the collective realm of story and storytelling. This produces a global consciousness of connectivity, not a power structure based upon a zero-sum game or an either/or divisive system of oppression.

One of the ways we can legitimise the story of human connection and interaction is to overcome the prevalent belief of opposition – that experiences are either one way or the opposite way, with *no* consideration of what lies between.

Binaries are a system of numbering or arguments that consider two parts of a whole. We live in a Western cultural paradigm where dominant binaries can largely create division and opposition and, as a result, occlude a diversity of voices. According to this model, people fall on an upside or downside on every issue. What if there were more to life than two opposing stories? What would that freedom look and feel like?

The mid-twentieth-century French philosophers and linguists Roland Barthes and Claude Lévi-Strauss devised a way to understand language and meaning through what they called *binary oppositions*. They observed how we have come to understand the meaning of specific words through their opposites more than through the word itself.

For example, understanding the concept of *winning* is only possible through the opposing idea of *losing*. Words can be viewed as symbols of society, and are largely based upon relationships of meaning. Language, in this sense, has the power to alter attitudes and behaviours.

This approach would also apply to other words, such as considering what is *good* based upon what we deem as *bad*. To feel *good* there must be a *bad*. If *good* people exist, the logic goes, then there must be *bad* people. But if the definition of *good* people is based on one story or a person's culture, education, and experience (CEE), then who decides who are the *bad* people? As we can see, this is a slippery slope that leads to oppressive belief systems and forms of discrimination discussed in the previous chapter.

Our adopted beliefs may influence our values so that we accept binary truths, such as *we are either winners or losers* or *I'm a loser if I lose my job*. But, in actuality, our values can thrive in multi-dimensionality beyond either/or language paradigms.

Blake teaches this in *The Marriage of Heaven and Hell*. We all succeed and fail together, and to survive and thrive in a free society we need to build language that supports *collectivity and relationships* instead of *opposition and isolation*.

Reframing language

The language we live by holds immense power over not only how we speak but also how we think and experience others. Language is the vehicle to understand and negotiate the many persistent binary oppositions in our everyday lives.

Judgement and criticism often result from binary or dualistic thinking by creating opposition to other people and to situations unfamiliar to us. Binaries are typically perceived as hierarchical oppositions, with one superior to the other. This produces the concept known as *othering* – where one part of the binary becomes subordinate to the dominant part (see Figure 4), such as the belief that one race or gender is superior to another or an *in/out* or *us/them* mentality.

In the current culture of fear, demonising the *other* as the *enemy* is a tool used to continually drive social division. This contributes to dehumanising each other and, as a result, accepting unacceptable and discriminatory behaviour. Rather, we can strive for change ourselves, or support leaders who avoid oppositional framings and who have the courage to advocate for equality. The language we use is significant in this process.

Oppositional framing relies on comparison and often results in stereotypes or scapegoating. Comparisons and generalisations emerge from oppositional language and

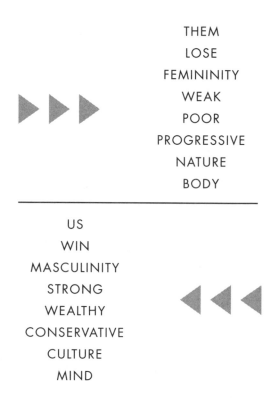

THEM
LOSE
FEMININITY
WEAK
POOR
PROGRESSIVE
NATURE
BODY

US
WIN
MASCULINITY
STRONG
WEALTHY
CONSERVATIVE
CULTURE
MIND

Figure 4: Stereotypical binary oppositions drawn from the traditional belief systems of patriarchy in the Western sociocultural context (see Chapter 4)

reductive thinking, much of which results from living only in our rational minds. However, conscious perception views the world through relationships, integration, patterns, and processes instead of reductive binaries.

Conceptual systems influence how we think about and perceive reality. When we *consciously* perceive, we lay the groundwork for rewriting our stories using imagery, intuition, and creativity. Part of this process involves the ability to notice without judgement, thereby eliminating divisive behaviour.

As the modernist novelist F. Scott Fitzgerald noted, 'The test of a first-rate intelligence is the ability to hold two opposing ideas in the mind at the same time and still retain the ability to function.' Observing thoughts as a *unity of oppositions*, instead of separating them as a dualistic binary, opens the doors of perception to infinite possibility.

Taoist and Yogic philosophies in China and India, respectively, consider the union of opposites integral to understanding existence. The Taoist Yin/Yang symbol has served as one of the most iconic images throughout human history (see Figure 5). While appearing to be divided into two parts, it wanes and waxes like the moon between many cycles – lesser *yang* (light) meets greater *yin* (dark), eventually moving to greater *yin* meeting lesser *yang*. At any point in the cycle, there is always a fluid dance between both sides.

Figure 5: Yin/Yang symbol signifying the union of opposites

Yin/Yang is more than just a symbol. It is also a philosophy illustrating the complex union of opposites, as does the practice of yoga – with postures creating simultaneous tension and relaxation in every moment. These philosophies work differently than binary opposition by demonstrating how the evolutionary processes of cycles and change blend into each other and cannot be separated into arbitrary divisions. As individuals and societies, we consist of a constellation of opposites finding union through (rather than in spite of) our differences.

This unification allows us to see multiple perspectives and possibilities through which we can view our own stories. We are not tied to one singular truth or account of our lives, or even the opposite of a truth we are rejecting. We can embrace many versions of ourselves, all equally valid, from which we can choose our preferred stories or explore new ones. We can also have compassion for our older stories rooted in other beliefs and allow space for them to change.

The binary principles of language fail to capture our ever-changing experiences. Limiting our language, we restrict our ability to engage with a wider conception of the world. Perhaps this is why the American social activist, writer, and teacher Dr bell hooks diagnoses how 'language is also a place of struggle'.

How can we consciously perceive beyond our limitations without a language to understand how to do it? This results in our inability to construct stories that empower us, building love and compassion, and, on a more social level, supporting freedom and equality.

The power of language depends upon the values and beliefs society places on it more than the actual meaning of the specific words themselves. The social psychologist Dr Kenneth Gergen's research on social construction shows how words have no *essential* meaning, because meaning is created in the moment of utterance – the time when words are spoken and heard. The process of doing and living language is the meaning-maker. Words acquire meaning in relationship when we use them to communicate with each other.

The primary reason for discussing binary oppositions in this chapter has been to illustrate how the ordinary language we use exerts significant influence over our perceptions and sense of ourselves and each other. Simplifying this even further, language matters – particularly storytelling and building new stories. Meaning, and how we make sense of the world, depends upon how language is learned, framed, and perceived, as well as who controls the overarching narrative constructed out of language.

Thinking too much

The primary storyteller controlling our fear stories is our own dominant mind. Society's penchant for privileging the reductive mind and using rational intelligence and knowledge production can limit many experiences. Such a mind narrates many stories that are false, and which stem from constructed beliefs external to us. When we accept these stories, it hinders our capacity for self-care and well-being because the stories are often rooted in fear.

I suspect many of us can agree that *we think too much*. It is one of the great challenges of the modern world. As Gergen explains in his book *Relational Being: Beyond self and community*, not only do we overthink, we also believe that the cognitive ability to think rationally and analytically serves as the *only* mode of interpreting, analysing, or perceiving the world around us.

Fortunately, the mind only represents *one* tool in an expansive and limitless toolbox of perception and understanding. An ancient Chinese proverb states, 'The mind is an excellent servant but a terrible master.' Western culture has a history of privileging cognition and reason as a master narrative and the only form of intelligence and interpretation.

The Age of Enlightenment of the eighteenth century and beyond, also known as the Age of Reason, prized rationality and logic over all other forms of intelligence and experience. Such a sociocultural response was intended to confront tyranny and ignorance perpetuated by corrupt ruling systems (monarchies) in collaboration with institutionalised religion through the monolithic structures of the church. By separating church and state, which was one major aim of the Enlightenment, ideas of individual liberty and democracy could be achieved alongside religious and cultural tolerance.

Prior to this revolutionary watershed in philosophy and intellectual reason, science and rational thought were dismissed, suppressed, and, at times, punishable by death. Such thinking, especially if it opposed those holding power, would often be shut down. Despite such opposition, science and rational thought heralded monumental progress in society, resulting in expansive forms of democracy, social equality, and medical advancement.

This is partly why the seventeenth-century French philosopher René Descartes set out in his book *Discourse on Method* to find the ultimate philosophy of knowing why we exist and how we think. Descartes' conclusion has become one of the most famous dictums in the Western world: 'I think, therefore I am / *Cogito, ergo sum*'.

As this proposition suggests, Descartes became obsessed with reductive thinking, what might also be called mechanistic thinking, where rational knowledge and understanding emerges from dividing objects or people as separate and individual parts of the whole. In their independent isolation, according to this approach, such parts can educate us about the nature of reality, thinking, and experience. For example, we can only know the nature of time by taking apart a clock and looking at the pieces.

Another name for this is *Cartesian dualism* (from the Latin for Descartes: *Cartesius*), which in large part produces a culture where binary oppositions (either/or) not only exist but also produce most of our social meaning. This applies to the separation of mind and body, or *mind-body dualism*, which has not served psychology or medicine well because it separates physical health and mental well-being instead of recognising their interconnectedness.

There are many benefits to reductive mechanistic thinking that continue to serve us today, such as evidence-based practices in engineering and science, but there is another detrimental effect: a legacy of overthinking and an overreliance on one type of intelligence or experience.

> One major challenge is our capacity for and reliance on excessive thinking.

Despite having many social benefits, reductive and rational thinking constitutes a single way of perceiving the world, and through its influence on the Enlightenment it has also influenced how so many of our education and social systems function today. As we will discuss in the following chapter, other paradigms beyond reductive thinking exist and are essential to addressing many of the issues produced by a culture of fear.

As a conclusion to this chapter and a transition to the next, let us close with a perspective from Albert Einstein – a convincing figure who strikes a balance between the reductive and rational, on the one hand, and intuition and perception, on the other. He stated, 'I believe in intuition and inspiration.

Imagination is more important than knowledge. For knowledge is limited, whereas imagination embraces the entire world, stimulating progress, giving birth to evolution.'

Shifting our paradigms has the power to transform who we are and how we live. It also allows us to advance the societies we ultimately learn from and to create through the building blocks of storytelling, such as intuition and imagination. Part of this process involves reimagining and reprogramming the stories of our lives, which often relies on tools outside of familiar modes of rational intelligence and knowledge production, and that will be explored in the next chapter.

REFLECTION QUESTIONS

How often do you allow yourself to shift your perception of the world and consider completely different paradigms?

Do you perceive the world in binary oppositions: right/wrong or good/evil? If so, does it produce joy, fear, or other emotions? Does it affect how you perceive those around you?

Do you struggle with excessive thinking? If so, how does this phenomenon increase anxiety or fear in your life?

CHAPTER 6

Intuitive Learning

Multiple intelligences

This chapter explores how we can alter some of our perspectives and ways of being in the world – from a place solely guided by the rational and reductive mind to one encompassing other forms of intelligence, such as emotional, observational, and somatic, as well as drawing on intuition in order to adopt tangible tools in our personal storytelling practice. Intelligence here functions as a way of understanding or knowing the world, a process that can be part of or exclusive to the brain. Story, similarly, influences many forms of learning and intelligence.

The educational psychologist Dr Howard Gardner promotes the concept of multiple forms of intelligence beyond the intellect of the mind. In his book *Frames of Mind: The theory of multiple intelligences*, his list of possible intelligences ranges from linguistic, logical-mathematical, and spatial, to musical, bodily-kinaesthetic and interpersonal. This research reflects other non-Western modes of knowledge transmission that have existed for millennia in other cultures and traditions. While a growing movement exists supporting teaching and learning through multiple intelligences, entrenched social and educational systems continue to influence our limited modes of perception.

We now live in a progressive time when there needs to be more balance between rational thinking and intuition, sensation, and other forms of intelligence. Indeed, such learning could serve as a new era of *intuitive enlightenment*, building upon our past advances in science and social progress, while also adding to them by prioritising other forms of intelligence drawing on both Western and non-Western systems to generate complementary forms of knowledge and perception. These different epistemologies and ontologies – or ways of knowing, understanding, and being in the world – contribute to storytelling through meaning-making and future-making.

Unfortunately, many of us may rely on the rational mind more often than on the body. Why is this such a problem? It cultivates more fear and anxiety because the rational mind is only one tool to decipher, and communicate with, the larger world around us. Descartes' invocation of *I think, therefore I am* had one huge implication. It separated the mind and body, thereby creating a dualism or split in the value applied to alternative knowledge systems.

All parts of the body, including the rational mind, rely on each other. The physician and author Dr Deepak Chopra has called the body 'an instrument of awareness'. As a cohesive whole, the body functions as a primary communicator of stories.

We can continue to develop a symbiotic or mutually beneficial relationship between the mind and body, learning the interrelational experiences of using the whole-body system to guide our understanding. From this standpoint, *somatic, observational,* and *emotional* responses provide three useful examples of integrative and interconnected learning through different forms of *haptic cognition* (touch), *embodied cognition* (mind not only connected to the body, but the body connected to the mind), and *distributed cognition* (the social and cultural contexts of knowing).

Somatic intelligence

Somatic intelligence (SI) views the entire body as an organism and relies upon our body's responses to communicate or receive information about our sensations and emotions, such as pain, joy, suffering, or sadness. Shifting our perception to draw on the intelligence of the somatic body and therefore sensory experiences and sensation is one way to shift the domination of the mind.

Our bodies are intelligent systems of interpretation and observation that communicate with and also provide information about people, places, situations, and experiences through other forms of intelligence such as intuition and observation. The senses of the body (sight, touch, taste, sound, smell), as well as myriad sensations we experience through the senses, are multidimensional complex systems of interpretation and multi-perception. SI draws on a range of body responses to deal with our internal and external needs.

In *A Natural History of the Senses*, Dr Diane Ackerman clarifies that we cannot understand the world without using all of our senses. But in the digital era, humans rely on vision 70 per cent of the time, with the remaining 30 per cent filled with other senses, primarily auditory (sound) and haptic (touch). Since the body receives input first, we can listen to this first line of response and process the feelings around it.

The senses function as the border of our bodies and are instrumental in how we process the world. Ackerman adds that, because 'our senses define the edge of consciousness', we are 'both explorers and questors after the unknown', where we are 'willing to risk our lives to sample a new taste' or experience a new sensation. Even though our bodies negotiate known and unknown worlds, we believe the mind ultimately controls the data received by the senses through the stories it narrates. We do, however, have options for how to narrate past, present, or future lives.

Hippocrates, credited as the originator of Western medical practice and ethical behaviour in healing and medicine, once claimed: 'There is a measure of conscious thought throughout the body.' Anishinaabe author Richard Wagamese takes Hippocrates' observation to another level. Beyond the mind, he acknowledges the connection between body, truth, and healing, particularly when he allows himself to feel the body: 'I become who I am – energy and spirit. I am not my mind. I am not my brain. I am stardust, comets, nebulae and galaxies. I am trees and wind and stone. I am space. I am emptiness and wholeness at the same time.'

As Wagamese expresses beautifully through somatic recognition filtered through non-Western Indigenous medicine, our relationship with our bodies, and subsequently with our senses, energy, spirit, and so on, forges unity with the cosmic whole. For example, the body often acknowledges a physical or an emotional ailment long before an official medical diagnosis. It can also do the same with trauma or memory lodged in the body.

Ultimately, SI unlocks some of the barriers created by the mind and opens possibilities for further knowledge about how we communicate with ourselves and others. Many practices already draw on SI to improve our body awareness, including yoga, dance, qigong, meditation, tai chi, and other forms of movement or sensation therapy.

Observational intelligence

The twentieth-century Eastern philosopher and teacher Jiddu Krishnamurti believed that the highest form of intelligence is observation. Krishnamurti taught this insight before observational intelligence (OI) became more recognised in the Western world. OI is about witnessing the world around us without judgement or analysis in order to process information outside of our immediate or past lived experiences.

Because people are constantly learning from their environments and gaining feedback from this process, observation serves as a crucial aspect of this learning and raises a few questions for consideration.

- How do we gather and process information from the people and situations around us?

- How can we engage in this process without influence or judgement from our own experiences and biases?

- How can we assess this information and then integrate it into our own learning process as a way to increase our own levels of intelligence?

Observational intelligence draws on our abilities to listen to and observe stimuli outside of our immediate experiences in order to witness other people or cultures.

While employing tools of observation may seem commonplace, such tools are often absent in a world of passive learning where people can acquire any information from the internet. Using OI becomes increasingly important in isolated societies rife with siloed groups, with confirmation biases or filter bubbles decreasing our exposure to experiences or ideas outside of our own known realties (see Chapter 5).

From a storytelling perspective, OI increases our ability to rewrite our own stories due to an increased understanding of other people's stories through observation. We can learn from other people's experiences through *their* observations, in order to increase our understanding of, and empathy towards, difference in ourselves. In fact, one of the steps to changing our belief systems outlined in Chapter 4 is learning to live beyond fixed systems of experience and knowing. Using our observational intelligence starts this process.

Emotional intelligence

Many of us will be most familiar with emotional intelligence (EI). In many ways, there is overlap between OI, SI, and EI because they all rely on non-rational ways of engaging with and perceiving the world.

EI is the ability to understand and communicate through a range of emotions, and to gain knowledge through empathy. EI enhances our ability to perceive emotions both in ourselves and others. In *What We Know about Emotional Intelligence*, Drs Moshe Zeidner, Gerald Matthews and Richard Roberts isolate some of the defining characteristics and benefits of EI:

- Identifying emotions in ourselves and other people through facial, voice, or physical cues.

- Understanding the causes and consequences of emotions.

- Learning how to regulate intense emotions, such as anger, sadness, and fear, to improve our physical and mental health.

- Assessing emotions to facilitate thought and other day-to-day functions.

These characteristics draw on earlier research on EI by the psychologist Daniel Goleman. In his book *Emotional Intelligence: Why it can matter more than IQ*, Dr Goleman presents five concise components of EI.

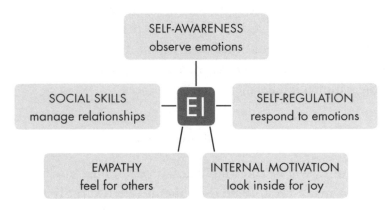

Figure 6: Goleman's five parts of emotional intelligence

As Goleman outlines, all five aspects of EI require forms of reflection and empathy that consider how we function in the larger sociocultural context. EI unlocks some of the barriers that we all face in our daily lives.

EI can be difficult to explain because, in terms of complexity and scope, our emotional landscapes are vast. Turning again to the Anishinaabe storyteller Wagamese, he suggests that the most important question to ask ourselves is not *What do I think?* but rather *How do I feel?*

This simple question invites us to consider alternative intelligences outside of the dominant mode of understanding the world: the mind. But *How do I feel?* can be a challenging question to explore and answer. Even the concept of *feeling* is often considered pejorative in a patriarchal belief system (see Figure 3).

At this point in the book, we know that demonising the process of *feeling* is a fictional story that continues to limit our capacity, as peoples and societies, to value emotional sensibility and its role in our lives. An awareness of emotional intelligence can enhance not only our interpersonal relationships, such as those within family dynamics, marriage, or work environments, but can also expand our own capacity to understand the layers of stories attached to the deeply held beliefs we carry with us.

Our intuitive sense

One of the major tools used in SI, OI, and EI is intuition, but few of us consciously access and use our intuition. It often lies dormant except for moments of acute awareness in our lives. With just a little bit of attention, however, we *can* begin to access the power of intuition that is within all of us.

Albert Einstein acknowledged how intuition is a 'sacred gift'. He observed: 'The rational mind is an obedient servant. We have created a society where we honour the servant and have forgotten the gift.' Intuition relies on our body's sensorial, emotional, and observational responses, among others, which produce deeper levels of perception of the world around us. Our intuitive sense, or our way of understanding what cannot be cognised or rationalised, ultimately assists us in overcoming our entrenched belief systems fuelling the fear-based stories that create suffering.

Intuition remains a difficult concept to understand. Unfortunately, dominant Western culture rarely advocates for people to cultivate intuition, as evidenced by standardised education systems that promote rote reductive learning based upon test-taking and memorisation rather than dynamic forms of intelligence. Picking up on Einstein's claim, society continues to struggle with the sacred gift of intuition. Regardless, intuition serves as a crucial part of our creative storytelling process because it draws on abilities beyond the rational mind to locate ideas, experiences, or circumstances outside of our otherwise limited cognitive abilities.

To put it more poetically, as Hermann Hesse has done in his poem about intuition titled 'Steps', 'the heart must submit itself courageously to life's call' and 'a magic dwells in each beginning'. Intuitive creative storytelling recruits the heart and evokes the magic of new beginnings that transport us beyond the rational and reductive to intuitive and expansive possibilities.

Now that we have considered intuition more generally, what is it exactly? The basic definition describes intuition as a process of understanding something without a rational account of it, or as the ability to access information through unconscious knowledge or cognition. I am sure we all have examples we can think of immediately from our own experiences in life.

One of the most useful ways of accessing intuition or explaining it is through direct experience – what in educational theory is called *experiential learning* through our lived experiences. While evidence of intuition remains experiential more than rational or analytical, there are many anecdotal accounts of intuition from credible sources.

Apple's founder Steve Jobs described intuition as 'more powerful than intellect'. Jobs was on to something, because intuition can elevate people to realms of extreme intelligence, forging together the power of ideas, creativity, and dreams, along with other forms of intelligence, to form a comprehensive system of human experience. Perhaps this explains why there are many quotes about intuition from Einstein, Nikola Tesla, Marie Curie, and other notable scientists and inventors.

Even the United States military acknowledges the power of intuition and applies it to its training to enhance the judgement of troops in combat. The programme manager at the Office of Naval Research, Ivy Estabrooke, maintains there is significant evidence to suggest that intuition is critical to how humans interact with their environments and how they make decisions in extraordinary circumstances.

Broadening this definition further, we might consider intuition as a way of sensing ideas, emotions, thoughts, and actions in ourselves and others. It is a method of listening to the somatic signals in our body, leading us to a certain path, course of action, or way of experiencing outside of our socially accepted sphere of mental perception. Intuition is a form of communication, or language, with ourselves, other people, and even the non-human world.

Can you think of a time when you knew something to be true? You could feel it in *your bones* – which is to say, you *knew* something that was unexplainable to your rational mind. Perhaps you knew someone was lying to you. Or you might have perceived of a future event that eventually became true. Maybe at work you made an important decision based solely on a *hunch*.

To clarify a common misconception, intuition is not the same as instinct. Slipping on ice and catching yourself from falling relies on instinct. When a car runs a red light, if you are able to veer out of the way, it is because of instinct. Relying

HAVE YOU EXPERIENCED INTUITION?

- Have you ever perceived someone's thoughts or intentions so clearly that it seemed surreal or out of the norm?

- Have you been able to know what someone else is thinking before the words are uttered from their lips?

- When a stranger enters a room, do you suddenly feel inexplicably drawn to or repelled by them?

- Have you sensed that an event will happen before it occurs?

- Do you sometimes experience other people's feelings almost as if they are your own?

on immediate reaction, instinct is often a fight-or-flight body response to a situation. Intuition, by contrast, draws on a different source of intelligence that is not reactionary or instinctual, but something cultivated through conscious practice and attention to a deeper field of knowing.

We often refer to this *knowing* as a *gut feeling*. Such a sensation is more than a feeling. It is an anatomical truth. Research has identified another 'brain' of our body in our *gut* or abdomen (gastrointestinal system).

In his book *The Second Brain*, Dr Michael Gershon explains how the enteric nervous system (comprised of the oesophagus, stomach, and large and small intestines) supplies a large number of cells that receive and send signals independent of the head brain. What Gershon calls the 'gut' or 'second brain' can often communicate emotional responses more accurately than the head brain because the *gut feelings* result from our body's intuitive language.

Teachings about the second brain range from Taoist alchemy and qigong (called the *dantian* in both) and Indigenous knowledge systems, to contemporary Western medical practitioners drawing on microbial health in the gut. For example, Dr Tyson Yunkaporta, who is a professor from the Apalech clan in north Queensland, Australia, acknowledges how *ngangk pi'an* is a term in Aboriginal language for an independent nervous system in the 'gut' – or another non-Western name for the second brain. This is a place housing our 'large spirit' or a higher intelligence. As Yunkaporta explains, the energy in the gut is widely held in Aboriginal traditions to significantly influence a person's health physically, emotionally, and spiritually.

Second brain research in both Western and non-Western systems highlights the relationship between gut health and our modes of emotional understanding and communication, both within our bodies and outside of them. While intuition serves as a larger process of accessing ways of knowing from non-rational sources, the second brain example illustrates other ways of proving that such knowledge systems outside of the head brain not only exist, but also might unlock a vast range of understanding about ourselves and the world around us.

Being more aware of our intuition allows us to function outside of entrenched belief systems and scarcity stories, opening us up to other possible paradigms.

Even though many of us do not consciously engage in this process because we have not been trained to do so, intuition sometimes appears randomly in our everyday lives through an occasional hit of insight or impression beyond our dominant senses. Imagine having the potential to not simply *trust your gut*, but to use your intuition actively to help guide your life choices and interactions in your relationships.

We can use intuition to observe our yet unrealised and un-written stories through the white noise of learned belief systems. Once we address, unlearn, and transform our socialised beliefs, we can then hear our desired stories more clearly. Fear is also a significant impediment to accessing our intuition. By reducing our fear narratives, we can also enhance our intuition. It is a mutually beneficial and symbiotic process, and a key part to shifting our overall paradigms.

Expecto patronum

Much like the students and elder wizards portrayed in the be-loved Harry Potter books (and films), our own *magic* abilities largely emerge from our intuitive abilities. Hermione Granger, although far superior in her mental knowledge to her fellow pupils at Hogwarts, only begins to truly understand magic once she can connect to her intuitive intelligence more than her reductive mind.

When we first meet her, Hermione relies on her mind for much of her decision-making and subsequent behaviours. While she benefits from her mind, she also experiences drawbacks. She is steeped in worry and insecurity, until she learns how to follow her intuition and combine it with her immense cognitive abilities.

Harry Potter, who is the opposite of Hermione, immediately shows an aptitude for magic – despite rarely studying or knowing anything about it – largely because of his unconscious reliance on intuition. Returning to Hesse's poem 'Steps', Harry submits himself to 'life's call', even amidst his own fear of what that might entail. Rather than being guided by his mind, he follows his intuition, despite the danger he constantly must confront.

If we look at this relationship more closely, Harry and Hermione represent two parts of ourselves. They symbolise the beneficial interplay of both the analytical and intuitive 'brains', demonstrating how both are necessary in our development, along with Ron Weasley, who represents the trickster element of curiosity and unpredictability. Harry and Hermione are extreme examples of each other, two parts of the whole, much like in the symbiotic relationship between Arthur Conan Doyle's iconic duo Sherlock Holmes and Dr John Watson. Mirrored successfully by their professor Albus Dumbledore, Harry and Hermione need both the rational and intuitive elements.

We can learn about intuition through our stories before applying it to the larger narrative of our world. Perhaps this is why J.K. Rowling discussed in her book *Very Good Lives: The fringe benefits of failure and the importance of imagination* how some form of external magic is not needed to transform the world because we 'carry all the power we need inside ourselves already'. Magic, then, is only a metaphor for the intuition we already carry.

The *magic* of our intuition serves as the ineffable process of our storytelling and retelling – or, in Hogwarts wizarding terms, casting and dispelling magic to alter known reality. Intuition assists us in using the Patronus Charm (Expecto Patronum) – as a wizard would do when invoking a spirit guide as a positive energy force to defend against the Dementors (who feed on human happiness and creativity) – on our learned belief systems in order to pave the way for us to relearn new stories.

Chapters 4 and 5 contributed to our understanding of the belief systems, dominant paradigms, and discourse that underlie a culture of fear. The principles discussed in this chapter explained how we might interpret the world around us, not only through the rational and reductive mind, but also through other forms of emotional, observational, and somatic intelligence, as guided by intuition.

This chapter also expanded upon these ideas to look at shifting our paradigms through alternative perspectives and experiences in order to start learning and writing new stories, which will be the subject of chapters 8 to 10. Before that, however, we will consider ways to accept and surrender in order to prepare for the storying process.

REFLECTION QUESTIONS

How often do you rely on other forms of intelligence, such as somatic, observational, and emotional? When placing awareness on your body, for example, do you feel less fear in your life?

Do you consider yourself an intuitive person? How often do you consciously use intuition? In what ways? Can you think of a time when you knew something to be true through an intuitive process?

CHAPTER 7

Acceptance and Surrender

Accepting impermanence

We have all been told to just *chill out* and *go with the flow*. While there may be some value to these suggestions, they are often used to minimise or even ignore our feelings, sensations, and experiences. Flowing with belief systems that are not our own must remain our choice and part of the stories we value.

This chapter proposes that sometimes we have to make space for external narratives in our stories by adopting positions of both acceptance and surrender. This process reduces the stress and tension caused by constant resistance, and frees us to practise yielding by redirecting some of the dominant narratives that fail to serve or support our lives. Yielding also serves as an apt metaphor in this chapter because of the agrarian connotation of growth and sustenance through patience and cultivation. Anyone who gardens knows how much acceptance and surrender goes into it.

Teachings on acceptance and surrender have existed for millennia. The Buddhist principle of impermanence, which states that *the only constant in life is change*, revolves around letting go of our perceptions, control, and ego to embrace the unknown. Fear, of course, immediately bubbles to the surface when we practise accepting and surrendering to the impermanence of each moment in our relationships, ideas, or experiences.

Embracing impermanence is frightening because our ego mind cannot quite comprehend the process. Stories of fear are quickly written by our minds when confronted with the unknown:

What if something happens to my son Eoin on the way to school? That pedestrian crossing in front of the school isn't very safe and the volunteer wardens are only children themselves. What do they know about stopping traffic? My son doesn't follow rules. What if he runs out into the road? I couldn't live if something happened to Eoin!

Our fear stories go on and on, and the possibilities for negative outcomes are endless. This is where learning to surrender helps, particularly when we feel out of control, or rather, when we recognise that we do not have control over certain circumstances or people.

We can learn to *accept* impermanence by *surrendering* to the unknown, letting go of our fear stories so that we can accept other possibilities both within and beyond our comprehension. 'Move outside the tangle of fear-thinking', as the Sufi poet Rumi teaches. Move away from the 'tangle' of the mind to let go of those fear-based narratives.

Acceptance serves as the first part of this two-part process because it often begins externally. People can be consciously in a place of acceptance – a moment of presence and awareness amidst difficult circumstances. If someone steals your bicycle, you can accept or resist this reality, with the latter reaction creating more tension, stress, and fear. Either way, the action has happened, and the reality of the missing bicycle remains.

Our *reaction* to a past or future event is subjective. While we cannot undo the theft of the bicycle, we can reach a place of acceptance rather quickly because we have little choice about the outcome after the fact. We are accepting not only an event that has passed, but also the feelings that emerge out of the past action. Using observational intelligence from the previous chapter, we can observe and listen to our feelings without judgement or attachment.

Once we accept the action and our feelings, we can then sink deeper into a state of surrender – of *being* rather than *doing*. Surrender serves as a way of experiencing the world more generally rather than as a reaction to a specific action or outcome. We can surrender to a future with many possibilities, some of which include surrendering to experiences in the past.

ACCEPTANCE	YOU	SURRENDER
(past event or experience)	(in the moment)	(future with possibilities)

Figure 7: Timeline of acceptance and surrender (with special thanks to Paul Harris for the idea).

Another feature of surrender is its ability to overcome physical and mental obstacles. If you have ever tried moving a large piece of furniture up a flight of stairs alone and realise after the first couple of steps that it is a foolish idea, then you must first *accept* this new reality.

The *surrender* comes when you give up the idea that it has to be accomplished in the way you initially thought: *I'm capable, and I can do it on my own. Why would I need help?* Rather than taking on the individualistic belief that I do not need help, I can surrender to the story that I do need assistance from other people and allow any possible outcomes that may emerge.

Surrender is also the ultimate anti-stress response. In her book *The Ecstasy of Surrender*, the psychiatrist and empathic healer Dr Judith Orloff explains how the process of surrender increases the production of endorphins and serotonin in our brains, which in turn leads to heightened feelings of euphoria. The process of surrender feels exhilarating once we can deepen our understanding and experience of it, allowing us to live in peace, relaxation, and enjoyment.

The goal is to ease our fear and suffering through the practice of surrender. Living in a state of surrender cultivates peace, while living in fear fosters suffering and pain. We can always live in a state of surrender, whereas acceptance, as in the example of the stolen bike, is a state we may only experience as necessity dictates based upon external circumstances or events. Surrender simply presents another story we can begin writing and living now, and one that can alter our psychic and physiological states.

Yielding instead of resisting

Unlike its denotative or dictionary definition, surrender is not a loss or submission to an opponent. No winner or loser emerges from any hierarchical battle or match. The real fight typically involves our constant resistance to the flow of events in our lives that we oppose because of our fear stories.

Resistance is often the favoured response, not because it always serves us well, but because it can ignite what fear sparks in us: the fight. When confronted with a fight or a threat, we often respond in kind rather than yielding or surrendering to an alternative outcome. Part of this is because we like the familiarity of the fight, and the addictive cortisol we receive from it. It feels normal.

Neutralising the fight or opposition, especially when it is foisted upon us, reduces the collateral damage on ourselves and others. T'ai chi ch'uan (tai chi) is a traditional Chinese martial art and meditation practice that focuses on cultivating speed and power through softness. Master Cheng Man-ch'ing used to say to his students: tai chi educates people to *invest in loss*.

To invest in loss does not mean taking a hit or giving in. It teaches us how we must yield to the power of external forces and redirect the force (or fight) as a way to neutralise the threat rather than meet it head on, which can damage everyone involved (see Figure 8). Our loss, in this case, represents our ability to surrender in order to survive and address the threat, rather than respond with force through fear and resistance.

Figure 8: *Yielding and a Cat*, by Assi Ben Porat

When we engage in a fight by resisting through force, we create more strain and stress in our lives. This increases our fear. The challenge here is that resistance produces tension in our bodies, activating our nerves and producing strong chemicals of adrenaline and cortisol because our body thinks it is in a state of survival or fight-or-flight.

Sometimes in life we must fight and resist, especially when we are in immediate danger. But most of the time we engage in unnecessary resistance. We consciously participate in the figurative fight and prolong it because it is part of our socially constructed stories about who we are and what values we must support.

> *Rewriting our stories serves as a powerful way of yielding and redirecting fear rather than resisting it.*

Resisting arduous circumstances serves as a direct action of the flight-or-fight mechanisms of fear. When we resist, we can close off our connection to ourselves and to the world and others around us. To fight is to resist rather than invest in loss and surrender – that is to say, yield to the threat of fear and deflect or repurpose it.

When surrendering, we redirect the fight by turning our intention elsewhere, especially to a more quiescent place that does not attract conflict or fear. The paradox of yielding produces a result where everyone wins.

To flee and ignore a problem is another form of resistance. 'When you have to make a choice and don't make it', commented the nineteenth-century psychologist William James, 'that is in itself a choice'. Neither fleeing nor ignoring a problem functions as surrender. If our stories of fear – *I can't live without this person in my life and I'm lost if they leave me* – dominate our everyday lives, then these fear stories will also overtake us in a genuine crisis.

Let me illustrate with another example of resistance. I live in an older urban neighbourhood in Vancouver, with narrow streets and parked cars on both sides. When two cars in opposite directions drive down a street, one must find a spot to pull over for the other to get by. Sometimes drivers wait at the end of the block for the other car (or multiple cars) to drive all the way through when there is no space to pull over. Usually people will politely wait for the other car and then wave in appreciation at the end. It is Canada, after all!

But occasionally there is a standoff and neither car will concede the lane. In one specific example, two cars would not move for each other. The standoff began with honking. Next, the two *men* yelled at each other out their windows. Finally, they both turned off their engines and just sat there staring at each other from the driver's seat.

I watched for a few minutes in disbelief, thinking they would get sick of this charade and move on. But they did not. Who knows how long they sat resisting?

This simple anecdote shows a situation where neither driver would surrender because of a fear of failure and of losing the fight. The two drivers, despite seeming to be in a hurry, wasted time by refusing to move. Their resistance, or inability to surrender, forced them both to suffer unnecessarily. If we were to connect this to the larger belief system of patriarchy, which they were clearly exhibiting, we can see their oppositional beliefs about winning and losing, as well as competition, conflict, and power.

We often resist life's situations for years without first asking: *What do I actually want? Which stories do I want to live?* The beauty of surrender is that it allows us time and space to decide if an action is worth doing and if it empowers us and supports our well-being. Many of us are often stuck in the resistance stage. It feels like we are accomplishing something when we are actually exhausting our energy without making much progress. And, worse, we are creating more fear stories that cause us more harm.

What is also difficult about trusting the process of surrender is that it transcends time and circumstance. Because of the flux and elasticity of time, we can surrender to stories in the past, present, and future simultaneously in the present moment. Often experiences in our past haunt us in the present, which also contributes to constructing future fear stories. Our past stories dominate the present, particularly if we ruminate or catastrophise, as much as our future stories do.

Accepting and then rewriting those embedded stories in the moment is as much a part of surrender as releasing and rewriting fear-based future stories that do not serve us. Unlike acceptance, which is often what we have to do in a moment – such as in a crisis that demands our immediate attention – surrender becomes a state of being in our everyday existence. Rather than *do* surrender, we eventually *become* surrender.

Surrendering is a different story, a different belief system, and one we can decide to practise instead of fear. Surrendering allows us to choose among multiple future actions. The aim for us all is to surrender more each day, a process that will eventually become more habitual with practice. Noticing and then changing our fear-based stories will allow us to surrender in our lives and, in turn, surrendering will open emotional space and freedom to rewrite new stories built around encouraging belief systems.

Processing shame and guilt

As we work on acceptance and surrender, little doubts about these processes may emerge. Our fear of inadequacy may resurface as we confront our fear-based stories. Then, because shame and guilt so frequently accompany the fears of inadequacy ingrained in us from an early age in dominant negative narratives, we may even regress to fearing that acceptance and surrender are cowardice and capitulation in disguise. In other words, we can forget the liberation embodied in acceptance and surrender and instead feel shame and guilt. Practice in confronting fear, guilt, and shame is the path to liberation.

Distinguishing, questioning, and then changing our belief systems takes practice. Why is this process so difficult for most of us? The answer is simple: we are not typically educated about how to do this as children or as adults. We are expected to live exactly in the opposite way: blindly accepting all of the stories of our families, communities, or cultures.

When growing up, we are often taught that it is an honour to have specific beliefs, such as religious or political affiliation (or even early support for our favourite football club!), and that we should be grateful for them. We ultimately have to decide whether to accept or reject those belief systems when transitioning into adulthood and beyond. This conscious transformation, while less explicit in Western cultures, is part of our rite of passage process.

In some cases, our inherited belief systems provide sustenance and foundational learning. In many other situations, as discussed earlier, these beliefs are rooted in fear and oppression. Shame and guilt are two common unconscious tools used to reinforce inherited belief systems.

One of my narrative coaching clients Vivian is a first-generation Chinese Canadian. Her parents emigrated to Canada from China when she was young. Vivian was raised at the end of the Cultural Revolution in China, a period openly characterised by its resistance to Western intellectualism and individualism.

As a young, intelligent, and intuitive child, Vivian experienced shame, blame, and punishment for being a girl who wanted to receive an education. Her parents somewhat unconsciously retained many of the belief systems from the Cultural Revolution and perpetuated those narratives. These stories were continually taught to Vivian.

Vivian's main challenges as an adult in her relationships, as well as in her career, continued to be guilt and shame. Her cultural learning supported guilt and shame as a motivator for working. The drawback is that shame contains significantly more authority over our self-worth than guilt, even though they serve as two sides of the same coin. Both also link to our stories of fear.

The difference between guilt and shame impacts how we value ourselves. When we feel guilt, we often take responsibility for an action. When we feel shame, we cannot see ourselves as worthy. In her book *The Gifts of Imperfection*, Brené Brown defines guilt as *I screwed up* and shame as *I am a screw-up*. I particularly appreciate this distinction because it highlights behaviour (guilt) vs. identity (shame).

In the guilt story, our *actions* remain the focus. In the shame story, *we* are fundamentally the problem. There is a distinction between our actions or behaviours and who we are as people. The point is that our decisions in any moment do not define us. Understanding this simple concept serves as a key to unravelling many unwanted belief systems because they serve as stories influencing our behaviours rather than stories defining who we are as people.

For Vivian, guilt and shame became interchangeable in her story. Her parents' inherited cultural beliefs used shame on children to make them work harder and *make something of themselves*. It is understandable for parents to want success for their children, especially when they leave one country for another in order to improve their lives. The intention usually comes from parental love.

However, using shame as a way to motivate children can create a life of feeling inadequate and worthless. Vivian continues to struggle with the process of separating her feelings of shame from her identity, and particularly around her career, money, and relationships.

Vivian's story reveals a belief system that promotes self-doubt and inadequacy rather than empowerment. Because of these socialised beliefs, decisions in her life have been made based upon stories of fear: *I'm not good enough*; *I can't succeed*; *I have nothing to offer*. The insightful takeaway from Vivian's story is how the use of shame as a motivator produced the exact opposite result of what her parents intended.

In his playfully mystical and poetic fashion, Rumi pinpoints the tension between guilt and shame, often framed as 'wrongdoing', when he proposes a place 'out beyond any ideas of wrongdoing or rightdoing'. Once people get out of unwanted belief systems and accept and then surrender the control these belief systems have over them, they can find a place of freedom from fear.

Vivian's universally relatable story is rooted in deeply held beliefs and practices, ones fixed in 'ideas of wrongdoing' that thwart her empowerment and overall well-being. To change her story, Vivian revisited those beliefs and practices, identified them, and decided which ones served her and which ones needed to be revised or rewritten as different stories (see Chapter 10 for the stages of REWRITE). Because of the rewriting process, she learned to separate guilt from shame and behaviour from identity. Vivian's story models a process we can all learn from.

Although the distinction between who we are and how we act may seem slight, it is rather significant, particularly in the ways we perceive or value our self-worth, adequacy, or competence. We can, however, alter this process by questioning our belief systems and then rebuilding the stories that reinforce shame into ones that empower us. It all begins by shattering illusions built upon beliefs that generate fear stories.

When we engage in radical acceptance and surrender in our lives, we can experience greater well-being rather than fear as a regular state of being. Making decisions based upon the stories we have actively engaged in writing for ourselves is better than choosing stories based upon blame and shame. Surrender and acceptance remain integral in this process. All of these elements of experience and understanding support the storying process that will be discussed in the final four chapters.

REFLECTION QUESTIONS

Do you struggle with accepting actions that happened in the past? Can you conceive of ways in which accepting and then surrendering may open up multiple positive actions and feelings?

Can you think of one of your worst fears? Now imagine how you might respond if it were to happen right now. How would this feel different if you were able to surrender and could accept that fear as a story? How can you reframe that story through a process of surrender?

CHAPTER 8

Living Is Our Story

We are stories

Having now set the sociocultural scene connected to our patterned beliefs, this chapter reveals how our personal stories integrate into and are influenced by the larger tapestry of collective stories. Our stories are bound in a relational framework beyond the individual, while they are also personal to our experiences. While this might appear as a paradox, it shows how stories function, presenting the sociocultural and personal as interconnected ways of understanding.

The world consists of a constellation of stories. Societies, communities, families, and individuals rely upon them. Storytelling – building on our personal and social narratives – drives human existence. The environmental writer Barry Lopez notices how 'everything is held together by stories', while the novelist Salman Rushdie recognises that we are 'the storytelling animal', the only creature who uses stories to define and explain their existence. By embracing our 'storytelling animal', which Rushdie calls our 'lifeblood', we can cultivate education and empowerment to produce greater meaning and well-being in our lives.

> *Storytelling is our lifeblood and we cannot survive without it.*

Because our personal and shared stories overlap, we might consider the following questions before moving forward:

- What stories do we live by?

- Are these stories our own or from others?

- How can we learn from other stories to rewrite our own?

- How do we observe and accept other stories?

- Through all of this, how do we live our own stories?

In Chapter 1, stories are defined as real or imagined events sewn into the fabric of our lives through written and oral ideas or images. Now is the time to consider how collective and personal stories provide accounts or descriptions to make sense of the simultaneity of time: past, present, and future in a circular process. Whether temporal or spatial, our stories are immensely influential to our lives. We are our stories as much as we live by them.

Chapters 8 to 11 of this book survey how the power and pervasiveness of stories is key to reducing our fear and enhancing our ability to perceive greater possibilities in the world around us. As individuals, we narrate our own lives – even though our personal narrator is often unreliable because of its tendency to follow the belief systems that have been socially imprinted upon us.

Fictional fear stories

As outlined in chapters 4 to 7, how we perceive the world directly relates to how we encounter old stories and then reconstruct new ones. The following anecdotal story, drawn from a talk given by the late spiritual teacher Ram Dass, illustrates the challenges of distinguishing reality from fear stories, showing how our perceptions can drastically alter the stories we construct in real time.

It is a story about a person and a boat. The foggy haze is so thick that a person in a boat can barely see ahead. In the distance, they vaguely see another boat in their path and politely call out, 'I'm coming your way. Just wanted to make sure you can see me.'

There is no response from the other boat, which creeps closer in the fog. After a few minutes of silence and no action, civility succumbs to fear and the person yells, 'Hey, you will hit me if you don't move. Watch out!' Still, there is no response from the person in the other boat.

At this point, the person in the boat writes a fear story in their mind:

What is this person doing? They're going to hit me and we both may sink out here in the lake. The fog is so thick that no one will be able to save us. We may drown and die! This isn't the way I want to go. I just wanted to take an afternoon row on the lake, and now this. It's outrageous!

The other boat is closer now and the person frantically cries out one more time, 'HEY, GET OUT OF MY WAY!' Nothing happens and the boats eventually collide.

The person in the boat unleashes their rage on the other boat: 'What kind of irresponsible person runs into another boat on the lake? You could have killed me! How dare you!' As the person continues to frantically scream at the other boat, the fog peels back across the lake just enough to show that the other boat is empty.

The takeaway from this story is how our fear of the unknown creates fictional stories of fear. The person in the boat writes a story about how another person is responsible for their possible injury or death. Of course, this is just a story and not what actually happens.

The person in the boat represents any of us. The other boat signifies the literal manifestation of our fear through imagery so we can concretise the power of our fear narratives. We construct our own situations, our own oppositional boats ramming into us, based upon false perceptions. When we remove the fog shrouding our vision, we can then clear a path for rewriting our stories where there are no longer two antagonistic boats on the lake.

Real and imagined stories

Why is it important to visit our personal stories and rewrite them by revisioning ourselves in new ways? The simple answer is that stories serving the interests of others rarely sustain us at the same time. We probably want to avoid being the person in the boat yelling at the other empty boat whenever possible. And yet, we often find ourselves in this infuriating position.

The main difficulty we have with perceiving ourselves through narratives is that the distressing emotions we feel on a daily basis, such as fear, hurt, and disappointment, arise from the imagined stories that have yet to happen and likely never will. Entertaining these narratives, however, makes them all the more likely to occur.

When there is fear about an upcoming event, such as a job interview, the default position is to imagine the various ways in which the interview might happen. One storyline could imagine the interview as negative, as guided by our fear and anxiety. In this story, we might imagine how the interview committee will ask questions we do not know the answers to, which sparks our feelings of unworthiness or concerns about our ability to perform the position's duties.

Such a story, which is all too familiar to many of us, stems from our universal fear of unworthiness and inadequacy. These feelings lead us to think: *What if they find out I'm a fake? What if they see I'm not good enough?*

The reason the phrase *fake it till you make it* gets used so often is that many of us feel like impostors, even if we are totally competent and exude a warrior-like confidence. The danger with living a life built upon fear narratives is that we will jeopardise our capacity to *make it* because it feels like we are repeatedly *faking it*. Faking it is a behaviour we learn in order to disguise our deep inner fears.

IMPOSTOR SYNDROME

Impostor syndrome is the imagined feeling a person has when they believe they do not belong in a job, relationship, or social group because they are not good enough. This story arises because people struggle to perceive themselves as worthy of their abilities or accomplishments. They believe they will be revealed as frauds. Some of the most confident, high-level achievers feel the most vulnerable and inadequate beneath all of their successes. Impostor syndrome is common for a reason: we all experience it on some level when reflecting on our abilities or accomplishments.

The above fear story about a job interview does not manifest because we actually lack qualifications. It arises from fear-based emotions felt prior to the job interview and has nothing to do with how the interview may go in reality or our skills and experience. The irony is that we imagine the worst result because we are afraid and let that fear story take over. In this story, doubts about our worth and imagined inadequacies have already dictated the outcome, producing an almost magnetic attraction to this possible reality.

We could, however, write an alternative story about the same job interview, one in which, whatever questions the interview committee asks, answers come with ease and confidence. We are asked questions that draw on immediate expertise and experience. The interview feels comfortable and even enjoyable. We feel respected by the committee. The interviewers see us as an asset to the team and they will hire us within a week of the interview. In this rewritten story, confidence and self-realisation have dictated another outcome, shifting the feelings in the moment while also producing other possible futures.

Both scenarios have yet to happen, of course, but both stories are different methods of future-making that change feelings in the moment. The first scenario demonstrates an imagined outcome based upon fear. The second shows what might manifest from embracing possibility and opportunity, writing a potential outcome that provides a sense of ease and confidence in the moment. Even if the latter story does not lead to a job offer, it might present other options. For instance, the hiring committee may be so impressed that they create a new position or recommend you to contacts at a different company.

Considering another possibility, this process can produce positive results through envisioning and writing empowering stories. If, for example, we imagine excelling in the job interview – answering questions with ease and skill – then we can potentially manifest this future story *and* reduce fear and anxiety during the interview process. The converse is also true: thinking negatively about the interview – how the questions will reveal inadequacies – will likely illuminate that fear story, breathing life into an otherwise fictional scenario.

Both stories, and subsequent feelings about them, relate to an event that has not occurred. And yet, both stories have the ability to produce real emotions in the present moment. Our stories, many of which have yet to manifest, produce physical responses in our bodies that have a correlative psychological and emotional impact in our daily lives.

Think about all the time and energy we lose by investing in stories based on fear. Think about how this process depletes our energy and our motivation to imagine a different story, one that enhances our overall well-being. It is maddening. And yet, we all experience it daily.

These two stories only serve as illustrative examples, but there are many different stories we can imagine for any past, present, or future situation in which we can refocus the outcomes in order to improve how we might feel in the moment. When we write new stories in our life, many opportunities appear where there were no visible doors before.

It is our ability to write and rewrite past, present, and current stories that will alter how we live and experience the world. Understanding myth and metaphor serves as one way to access the symbolic language that helps us to visualise and create stories.

Metaphors of meaning

There are numerous archetypal stories that emerge from mythologies, which are stories that attempt to explain human existence. Such stories ask questions about who we are, where we come from, and what is the meaning of existence. Because myth comes from the Greek word *mythos*, meaning word or story, mythology could also be defined as the study of the human story.

What is important to recognise about myth and story is that they are symbolic and metaphoric in construction and meaning. For example, Harry Potter defeating the real Lord Voldemort, as well as the story of him told by others, could be any one of us confronting any of these seemingly insurmountable obstacles in our lives.

Our mythical experience, where story is the foundation of cultural and human experience, relies upon metaphoric language and aptitude. The Swiss psychiatrist and psychoanalyst Carl Jung observed how 'wisdom is knowing in depth the great metaphors of meaning'. Metaphor is the language of mythology and of storytelling.

Metaphoric language serves as a symbolic way of expressing complicated meaning through imagery and conceptual understanding to show comparison or connection. It functions as a form of perception we constantly use through language, word, and thought (e.g., *time is a thief*, *I'm feeling blue*, or *my heart is broken*). We enrich our language through creative figures of speech. Often considered a literary device reserved for romantics, poets, and writers, metaphor is actually a universal tool of perception that influences the ways we think and act in our daily lives.

For example, I might say in jest to my friend Michael, 'You are such a child', if he does something immature. I do not really think Michael has reduced his age by forty years. I am using humour or hyperbolic language as an exaggeration to prove a point. The metaphor is not the literal usage, but a figurative reference of greater meaning to provide a mental image or story people can remember or emphasise.

Our cognitive experience relies on our ability to decipher metaphor through language. Even the common phrase *war on drugs* is a metaphoric concept. It is impossible to literally stage a war, with tanks, soldiers, and bombs, to overcome addictions or halt the use of illicit drugs. The metaphor of war creates an extreme mental image of the problem. It is a divisive and fear-based metaphor because it is rooted in violent imagery, emphasising a combative and destructive solution to a complex human problem needing empathy and understanding to assist with prevention.

The war metaphor – also used in other contexts, such as *war on cancer, war on contagion, war on terrorism, war on immigration* – normalises violent and oppressive language in contemporary society. It illustrates a combative story of win/ lose or either/or opposition (see Chapter 5). Using metaphors invoking violence or winning/losing battles only exacerbates the situation. For example, such language adds to a family's distress when a member dies of cancer – as if the 'battle' was not fought hard enough.

War metaphors emphasise a culture of fear in which we live through their connotative language. Literal language is denotative (dictionary definition) and symbolic language is connotative – consisting of a range of meanings based upon the cultural or historical context. Metaphors are connotative in meaning, as are stories.

The challenge arises when we confuse the one-dimensionality of denotation with the multi-dimensionality of connotation. The meaning is then lost in the container in which the insight is intended to be found. If someone literally thinks human soldiers have been deployed to fight cancer in people's physical bodies, then the intended symbolic language – emphasising the enormity of the task involved in overcoming cancer – has been lost.

In their pioneering book *Metaphors We Live By*, cognitive linguist Dr George Lakoff and moral philosopher Dr Mark Johnson outline how the metaphors we use also shape our perceptions of the world and of other people, defining what we experience and then believe as truth in our everyday lives. In other words, we live conceptually and linguistically through metaphor. Although we may not consciously know we are thinking and speaking in metaphor, we are nevertheless doing so constantly. Similarly, we may not be aware that our stories are perpetually moving in our heads like a movie reel.

> *The meanings and understandings of language emerge from the conceptual framework of our interactive collective and personal stories.*

One of the main complications in contemporary society is that we often neglect to recognise the metaphoric foundation of existence and interaction. When we perceive language, story, or even religion as literal instead of metaphoric, much of the meaning and substance disappears. Symbolic language profoundly resonates through storytelling, and many influential spiritual teachers apply this principle.

The teachings of Buddha and Jesus are largely based upon metaphoric language. Jesus said, 'I am the Light of the world; he who follows Me will not walk in the darkness, but will have the Light of life.' Jesus does not become the sun or an actual spotlight in the sky. He uses the light/dark metaphor as a teaching technique to help people visualise internal states of being.

Jesus' teachings were never intended to be read like a newspaper, listing actual events and facts with historical accuracy. They are literary in approach, relying on the metaphoric language used in parables, allegory, similes, and images. These teachings become more poignant and transformative when interpreted through metaphor rather than through literalism because of how they magnify in perception and application.

I think it is safe to say that few people actually believe that when the sun rises each morning, it is literally Jesus in the sky. But it is easy to accept the metaphorical teaching of Jesus: how believing in love and tolerance shines greater light on humanity and improves the world and those people and animals within it.

Buddha similarly spoke in metaphor to understand complex meaning about ourselves. In one teaching, he said, 'The mind is everything. What you think you become.' This concept not only aligns with what is being discussed in this book – that is, we are our stories and our intention and intuition support this process – it is also a metaphor, not a literal statement. Mind and thinking, in this translated example, serve as mechanisms to imagine and perceive outside of our rational tendencies.

If we *think* we are a tiger, we do not literally *become* a tiger. By imagining ourselves to inhabit the qualities of a tiger, however, we might approach a goal at work with fierce tenacity and a hunting spirit. The image of the tiger supports our actions around what we want to become in a particular situation rather than literally growing fur, whiskers, and having paws the size of a human torso.

In the delightful book *Sand Talk: How Indigenous thinking can save the world*, Tyson Yunkaporta talks about how metaphors are really the language of spirit. They concretise the abstract in imaginative ways, ultimately bridging the gap between theory and practice. As we see from Jesus and Buddha, along with other examples from Indigenous traditions, they draw on metaphor to access the language of the spirit, those spaces outside of the rational intellect that themselves draw on universal stories or mythologies.

Seeing metaphors in each story does not limit the power they may have in our lives. In fact, it is quite the opposite. Literal interpretations remain one-dimensional, while symbolic language opens up many possibilities of meaning and future-making. When making important decisions, do people want only one limited option or many?

Mythology serves as a narrative, cataloguing collective histories, cultures, and values into complex forms of symbol and ritual throughout the world. It is no wonder, then, that myth has steered human civilisation for millennia. Universal themes return again and again through the power of story and metaphor.

This chapter has called on us to question our ability to consciously perceive that what matters to us directly relates to our stories, and offers methods for understanding how these stories might be more integrated through the ways we conceive of them. Adopting fear-based emotions associated with fictional narratives, whether our own or others', can lead to a number of problems, including illness, relationship issues, career uncertainty, and financial challenges.

A person's life is comprised of hundreds of thousands of stories. Our perceptions of these stories change depending on how we live our life (consciously or not), and how the larger social narrative is changing. After gaining insights in this chapter into myth, imagination, and metaphor that encompass living as story, the next chapter will consider how we might embody our stories by *being* them.

REFLECTION QUESTIONS

Have you ever been the person in the boat, mistaking fictional problems for your own? Are you still the person in the boat?

Do you often confuse metaphoric experiences for literal ones? If so, how does this change the story you tell yourself about these situations?

CHAPTER 9

Being Our Stories

Narrative empathy

Experiencing a story requires an ability to perceive, process, and self-reflect. As discussed in the previous chapter, many people have yet to acquire the skills to interpret and create stories using tools such as metaphor, imagery, or myth. This chapter encourages awareness of our story-making process, which involves introspection and reflection about who we are in connection to our communities and cultures.

Story-making allows active or *conscious* participation in the ways of *being in the world* – defined in philosophy as an ontology, or how we relate to and understand our existence. How we exist in the world, to ourselves and within our communities, remains dependent upon how we read or perceive the stories supporting our existence.

As a research professor of arts and humanities education, as well as a narrative coach, workshop leader, and public speaker, I have witnessed the power of story in our lives. I have studied its effect across different cultures and historical periods, as well as how narrative directly impacts people's lives. The result is quite simple: we constantly experience the world through stories and storytelling.

Watching a film, viewing social media, or reading a novel relies on the process of storying, drawing on the human experience to create entertainment that cuts deep to our core. As we witness other people's stories, we reflect more deeply on our own. In this way, our relationship to narrative and storytelling becomes reflexive, where our own stories are as important as witnessing other stories.

> *Experiencing other people's stories is deeply connected to our own storying process.*

We search out and consume stories not only because they reflect our own reality, but also because we actually enjoy watching and experiencing them. Dr Jonathan Gottschall explains in his book *The Storytelling Animal* that observing other people's stories resembles what flight simulators do for pilots. Citing the psychologist and novelist Keith Oatley, Gottschall outlines how stories serve as 'an ancient virtual reality technology that specializes in simulating human problems'.

Experiencing other people's stories enhances our ability to feel empathy for others and for circumstances outside of our own lived realities. Research confirms that a person's neural networks become activated when experiencing emotion. Perhaps this seems somewhat obvious. What is not so clear, however, is how we also feel stimuli in our neural networks when we observe other people experiencing emotion, whether real or fiction. We can feel other people's stories in our bodies as much as our own stories.

The literary researcher Dr Suzanne Keen characterises mirror neuron research as a theory of 'narrative empathy', where forms of story and storytelling enhance our ability to feel and relate to others. Keen explains that narrative empathy 'is the sharing of feeling and perspective-taking by reading, viewing, hearing, or imagining narratives of another's situation and condition'. This process can range from reading a novel or watching television to hearing about another person's experience through storytelling.

Because of the revelatory findings in mirror neuron research and narrative empathy, there are now neurophysiological

MIRROR NEURONS

The neuroscientist Dr Marco Iacoboni, whose work has focused on mirror neuron research since the 1990s, discusses how observing and understanding other people in visual and digital culture affects viewers. Mirror neurons are a collection of special cells found in the brain that imitate external actions. Iacoboni describes how the 'mirror neurons in our brains re-create for us the distress we see on the screen'. In his book *Mirroring People*, he further explains:

> We have empathy for the fictional characters
> – we know how they're feeling – because we
> literally experience the same feelings ourselves.
> … 'Vicarious' is not a strong enough word to
> describe the effect of these mirror neurons.
> When we see someone else suffering or in
> pain, mirror neurons help us to read her or his
> facial expression and actually make us feel the
> suffering or the pain of the other person.

Iacoboni's mirror neuron research clarifies why people constantly absorb all kinds of stories. Empathy is deeply engrained in our biology. For example, experiencing storytelling in digital culture (video, social media, streaming television, podcasts) through multisensory inputs engages empathy.

explanations for people's penchant for absorbing all kinds of stories, storying, and storytelling. We can feel empathy, along with other potent emotions, as virtual experiences when viewing stories separate from our own. Our brains function similarly whether we are feeling our own or other people's stories.

Perhaps this is why we are attracted to other people's fictional stories: to avoid the dramatic fear loop in our own daily lives. Maybe it is an escape. But it is familiar to anyone who experiences the power of narrative and how that can change our perception of ourselves or of other people and cultures.

What we know is that story remains ingrained in our lives, values, and psyches. If we are not living in our own stories, we are living in someone else's story, whether at work, within our family, on social media, or on television. We can begin making our own stories, however, and focusing on the present moment helps in this process.

Living moment by moment

Right now, this very moment, is our story. Every moment is an opportunity. As the American poet Emily Dickinson wrote, 'Forever is composed of nows'. We all have stories that are active, and that, with an influx of new energy and attention, can be rewritten. This is our choice every second of our lives and there are plenty of occasions to either revisit older stories or create new ones.

We have likely all heard of the clichéd phrase *live in the moment*. While clichés can oversaturate our language and reduce the effect of widely understood meanings, there are nevertheless truths in them. Despite what we think about the present moment, our physical bodies all live in the moment, drawing on somatic and emotional intelligence (see Chapter 6), even if our minds do not.

Being in the present moment is an integral process of examining and rewriting our stories. Our stories arise each moment; they can either appear as we have previously learned them or they can be rewritten. For the rewriting process to work, we must acknowledge our controlling belief systems rooted in fear and relearn our perspectives based on models of liberation and wellness, as explained in the first seven chapters of the book. Truly being in each moment, while also reflecting upon the past and future, remains an integral part of this practice.

The author and teacher Eckhart Tolle was catapulted to fame at the turn of the twenty-first century after his 1997 book *The Power of Now* was promoted by Oprah Winfrey. With millions of copies sold and translated into over thirty languages, the book's popular appeal magnified one major issue in society: that we have yet to grasp or appreciate the universal practice of living in the moment.

For Tolle, all difficult feelings and experiences result from living outside of the present moment: 'Unease, anxiety, tension, stress, worry – as forms of fear – are caused by too much future, and not enough presence. Guilt, regret, resentment, grievances, sadness, bitterness, and all forms of non-forgiveness are caused by too much past, and not enough presence.' Tolle tapped into the cultural zeitgeist because his teachings appeared at a time when fears about our futures and our pasts were increasing at an alarming rate.

Many other teachings about the present moment have been around for millennia, paralleling spiritual practices such as Christianity, Judaism, Hinduism, Taoism, and Buddhism, as well as other Indigenous traditions. Buddha, who was perhaps the most ardent practitioner of meditation, taught: 'Do not dwell in the past, do not dream of the future, concentrate the mind on the present moment.' Lao Tzu, the progenitor of Taoism, wrote: 'To the mind that is still, the whole universe surrenders. To be in the moment is the miracle.' Similarly, Jesus said: 'Therefore do not worry about tomorrow, for tomorrow will worry about itself.' Thich Nhat Hanh, the Vietnamese monk and author, recognises: 'Life is available only in the present moment. If you abandon the present moment you cannot live the moments of your daily life deeply.'

Other modern writers and teachers, not typically associated with spiritual teachings, also embrace the power of the moment. Leo Tolstoy, the great Russian novelist, offers this: 'Remember then: there is only one time that is important – now! It is the most important time because it is the only time when we have any power.' American psychologist Abraham Maslow wrote: 'The ability to be in the present moment is a major component of mental wellness.' Oprah, the ambassador of contemporary spiritual teachers and authors on her show *Super Soul Sundays*, reinforces: 'Living in the moment means letting go of the past and not waiting for the future. It means living your life consciously, aware that each moment you breathe is a gift.'

Most forms of spirituality or self-care practices talk about being in the present to improve our lives. Allowing ourselves to feel each moment, experiencing that stillness surrounded by life's persistent chaos, sounds simple. And yet, it is an ongoing

BENEFITS OF LIVING IN THE PRESENT MOMENT

- Slows down time

- Increases the ability to feel and perceive

- Enhances the body's senses and reduces the power of the mind

- Clarifies desires through conscious perception

- Reduces stress, anxiety, and fear

- Minimises shame or blame about past events

- Quiets inner voices of unworthiness and inadequacy

- Improves health, wellness, and well-being

challenge for humanity to embrace. While being in the present might be one of the most basic ideas to understand, it remains one of the most difficult to practise and sustain.

Whether acknowledged or not, everyone lives moment-by-moment, even if we cannot consciously experience it. The physical body sustains life based upon each breath and every beat of the heart. The physical, organic world, to which we all remain attached on some level through our bodies, reminds us of each instant.

Without the mysterious workings of the moment, particularly through the intelligence of our own bodies, we would all be dead. For example, the heart beats and the digestive tract moves food and nutrients throughout our bodies whether we think about it or not. The problem is we are not always aware of each breath or heartbeat in every moment. Our bodies, what we might refer to rhythmically as our *moment metronomes*, accomplish this on their own without conscious attention to breath or heartbeat.

What often happens in these moments, largely because we are already wired for storytelling, is that our mind continuously plays stories about the past, present, and future. Such stories are usually laced with a sticky, viscous layer of fear or anxiety. We invest in these fear stories, building our lives around them somewhere in the past or the future, while viewing the present as an extension of past or future fictions.

Practising being present leaves us vulnerable and disposed to intense emotions connected to our fears. The space we have created to observe the present quickly fills with thoughts, which are usually stories in our mental archive. Understandably, this presents a challenging paradox. The more we practise being present to the moment, the more we can understand our belief systems and patterns of perception in order to reduce the power of our fear stories.

And yet, we continually relive these older moments as though they are always in the now, much like in the Harold Ramis film *Groundhog Day*, where the protagonist Phil (Bill Murray) wakes up every day only to find himself trapped in the same day played over and over again. Even in the film, Phil eventually rewrites his character's story through experiencing every moment of one specific day again and again, to learn and relearn about socialised behaviour in order to become a better person. In doing so, he breaks the cycle of the perceived time warp, an unchanged loop that remains until Phil learns to live in and appreciate each moment.

While we experience the effects of fear in the moment, it is not the present moment causing our fears, but the story reels already running in the mind about a future scenario. We experience fear in real-time based upon fictional stories taking place in another time period, even though it feels like they are occurring in the moment.

Over time, as we practise witnessing *our present moment*, these stories from our mind will eventually fade. We can then write new stories of empowerment and well-being, a process that eventually becomes habitual. Allowing ourselves compassion and the knowledge that we are doing enough, much like in the story of Hummingbird below, will assist in the rewriting process.

No change is too small

'The Story of the Hummingbird', famously told by Dr Wangari Maathai, the Kenyan activist and 2004 Nobel Peace Prize laureate, also appears in other global Indigenous traditions. For instance, I first heard the version from the Quechuan people of South America, accompanied by Haida-manga illustrations (see Figure 9), through Michael Nicoll Yahgulanaas' account in the book *Flight of the Hummingbird: A parable for the environment*. The following telling blends the two versions.

One day there was a large fire in the forest and all the animals had to flee their homes. They went to the safest place they could: the river's edge. In shock and disbelief, they all looked on as the fire raged in the grove of spruce and pine trees. Bear, Wolf, Rabbit, Beaver, and other animals all expressed their sadness about losing their homes. Sitting in despair, they felt powerless in the face of annihilation.

The only animal who did not act this way was Hummingbird. As the animals squeezed along the river's edge for safety away from the fire, Hummingbird flew over and picked up a couple droplets of river water in her tiny beak and then rushed over to release the drops on the fire. Hummingbird then buzzed back to the river, collected a few more drops of water, and dropped them on the fire as before. This process continued a few more times while the other animals just sat and watched despondently.

Finally, Bear, the self-appointed leader and pragmatic voice, said to Hummingbird: 'Don't bother. It's no use. You're too small, your beak is too tiny, and these drops of water will not extinguish the fire.' Hummingbird remained undeterred by the enormity of the task and continued as before.

Figure 9: Haida Manga design of Hummingbird (Dukdukdiya) dropping water on the fire, by Michael Nicoll Yahgulanaas

The animals continued to watch. They looked defeated. Bear then insisted that Hummingbird stop this nonsense at once. He yelled, 'What are you doing? Why don't you stop?' Hummingbird, without pausing from the mission, looked back and declared: 'I'm doing what I can.'

As we know, personifying and anthropomorphising animals in this story is not meant to be literal. The story illustrates how each person (and animal), in their own small and seemingly insignificant ways, contributes to changing the world. This process begins with oneself, woven into smaller and larger global communities.

Despite society's apathy, symbolised by the paralysed animals waiting on the river's edge, we must carry on and do the best we can in each moment. We all rewrite the stories that eventually transform our collective stories, without fully understanding their potential impacts. This is the point: we must do storying; we must be our stories.

The metaphor of Hummingbird implies hope and courage in the face of fear. The metaphoric language and imagery in the story stresses the significance of one person not only to solve a problem, but also to show up, be present, and try, even in the face of failure. This is courage. It is showing up in moments of crisis.

The story teaches that all efforts matter, every drop of water contributes to the energy and momentum of global liberation and healing. Large movements begin with small grassroots gestures, such as tiny droplets of water on a blazing fire, to awaken collective support from others. Hummingbird is a story of hope. It represents everyone's potential stories. Every task infused with consciousness and intention becomes significant and transformative.

As Maathai expressed in an interview, particularly regarding her social justice and environmental activism, 'I will be a hummingbird.' In this way, the story broadens our scope, applicable to any situation. But it is also an environmental parable about the existential threat of climate change in contemporary times.

When confronted with troubles on a scale too large to conceive or understand, we often become paralysed with fear. Some issues are too great for the rational mind to comprehend, which is when fear stories fill the space. This should not stop us from *doing everything we can*, little by little, to remedy the pain and suffering of ourselves or others.

After all, failure does not signal losing. True failure rests in the inability to try at all. Failing is integral to our stories. Hope, tenacity, and resilience arise from our ability to accept our so-called failures.

As the Irish author Samuel Beckett reminds us, 'Fail again. Fail better.' What is interesting about this quote from his 1983 prose piece 'Worstward Ho' (a parody of Charles Kingsley's *Westward Ho!*) is that people usually only cite this last part. The full quote, 'Ever tried. Ever failed. No matter. Try Again. Fail again. Fail better', provides a larger picture of the process, demanding that we must show up to life, saying *yes* to the adventure of living and surrendering to our subsequent fears. Beckett captures how to embrace living and failing, both of which are equally important to *being our stories*.

Our personal stories resemble Hummingbird's story. We have the ability to reframe moments of fear in our stories to ones of empowerment and well-being. The effects will slowly take shape and will alter our personal lives and society as a whole.

Conscious storytelling and oneness

Conscious storytelling is living in the present, even if it might be about both the past and future. Time in this way is elastic, not static. Living in the moment helps us to transcend time and achieve ultimate surrender and contentment. But it is the synthesis of living in a cohesive temporal existence, not relying on entrenched stories of past and future to alter how we feel in the moment, that allows us to achieve liberation from our fears.

The story of the *now* draws on narratives related to all of us sharing the same experience. As individuals, our stories impact the world as much as the world's stories influence us. 'We are part human, part stories', as Okri recognises. This reciprocity contains multitudes, unending constructed belief systems about individualism removed from our sociocultural interconnection.

Framed a bit differently, let us consider how oneness is foundational to our existence. Which is to say, everything and everyone are all part of the same whole. Individuality, or separateness from each other and the whole of everything in the universe, is an illusion. Psychological research from Dr Kate Diebels and Dr Mark Leary found that people with belief systems rooted in oneness adopt a universal concern for the welfare of others.

Oneness is a way of seeing that people are all part of the same team, despite our superficial differences. Rather than striving for the illusion of individuality, oneness as a biding principle is one of the antidotes to fear. It also provides tools to heal societies that are fractured through, for example, political divisiveness and racial intolerance.

How we do storying and storytelling highlights and reflects that oneness. Within this context, we need to rewrite our stories of fear, shame, and unworthiness as much as we need to rewrite our collective stories about wealth inequality, human trafficking, social responsibility, and environmental violence. All are mutual and interdependent.

Knowing our connection to both ourselves and the larger collective remains vital to our healing. The world's problems are also our own, declared Krishnamurti, because 'we are the world'. The influence of a person's thoughts and actions, especially as they both appear in story, ripples across the waves of collective consciousness and eventually crashes on shores well beyond what the eye can see. We can view our stories collectively – through, for example, television, social media platforms, cultural stories about our histories, or mythology – as well as individually on a personal level.

The universal global presence of storytelling and narrative reinforces a deep and lasting collective human experience. The stories we live by do not exist in a vacuum, isolated from each other. Stories are as interconnected and interrelated as human relationships, environments, and cultures. We can all relate to the courageous Hummingbird, doing our best to find unification with our stories and those around us. We can be our stories every moment of every day.

REFLECTION QUESTIONS

Have you encountered emotional shifts, or even physical sensations, when experiencing another person's story, whether in real life or on film or television? How often are you aware of this process of narrative empathy?

How much of your day do you live in the present moment? Do you feel anxiety and self-judgement when not living this way? Does this prevent you from returning to the moment?

Do you struggle with failure? Can you see how failure is an integral part of your success? Think of one of your failures, especially the one you already think about too much, and reimagine it as a story of success.

CHAPTER 10

REWRITE Our Stories

The process of REWRITE

We now arrive at the pinnacle chapter, which presents practical applications through a process called REWRITE. To provide necessary context, the previous chapters of the book outlined the underlying principles, circumstances, and concepts to the practice of rewriting our stories. Up to this point, we have considered the authority and influence that storytelling has in our lives and how, when accessing it, we can transform our habits and attitudes by perceiving the world around us differently.

Figure 10: Seven-stage process of REWRITE (see also the Appendix for an accessible REWRITE chart)

Fear only has control over us insofar as it impacts our current stories, largely connected to our learned collective social stories. When broken down, fear is only one possible story in any situation occurring in the past, present, or future. Once we acknowledge many of our belief systems rooted in a culture of fear, we are given the opportunity to then shift the paradigm – or how we see and experience the world – before we can write new stories. Millions of other possible stories exist, waiting to be written or rewritten.

REWRITE is a series of seven stages that can be applied directly to our lives. The acronym REWRITE provides an easy device for remembering the stages of *rewriting* so that they can become habitual and effortless (see Figure 10).

Before beginning, take about ten or fifteen minutes and think about, reflect on, or write short answers to the following questions that correlate to the seven stages of REWRITE. It is a highly subjective exercise, so there are no right or wrong answers.

1. What are your stories and which belief systems guide them? How have people or groups in your life shaped these beliefs and your sense of identity?

2. How can you accept and validate your stories? How do they relate to other personal stories or social discourses? Do other people's stories often take priority over your own?

3. How do you witness your fears and link them to related belief systems? How do you feel when examining some of the dominating fear stories in your life?

4. What are your goals and the processes to achieve them?

How might these outcomes empower you and support self-care and well-being in your life? How could your desires coincide with other people, social groups, or communities?

5. Have you created new stories that will empower you? Have you co-created stories through relationships that support you?

6. How can you communicate versions of your stories until they replace former negative stories (i.e. learned belief systems)? To whom or to what groups of people do you feel uncomfortable telling your stories?

7. How can you cultivate more creativity in your daily life? How might these creative tools and activities enhance your aptitude for story-making and storytelling?

Recognise who you are

We begin with the most foundational stage in the process: *recognising* who we are in our own stories. Some of us may *think* we *know* who we are, but throughout this practice we will gain clarity on our identity and the stories that we have learned to believe about ourselves.

Or, in other cases, some of us have already changed our stories over time and have found ourselves in transition, confused about where we have come from, where we are now, and where we would like to be. One thing is certain: we never stop writing our stories. Let us now recognise and activate these stories.

In our professional and personal lives, we are increasingly expected to know our *brand* – how we define and sell our skills in the so-called marketplace. Linked to consumerist culture, people are portrayed as a product being bought and sold. Literally branding ourselves furthers the problem of connecting our salvation or worth to our labour in the socioeconomic system. Relying on stories of scarcity based upon the desirability of our personal brands stems from a culture of fear (see Chapter 3).

Branding illustrates the power of our personal, professional, and social stories in a rather diminishing way, reducing our *being* to a brand where our only value is based upon the number of likes, followers, or sales our brand attracts. The American artist and film director Andy Warhol sarcastically quipped how consumerist 'pop art' is all about 'liking things'.

Instead of thinking of our own brand, let us consider our own story. We are not *selling* ourselves, our *being*, but rather we are constantly *writing* and *creating* many versions of ourselves in the different contexts in which we live.

Recognising our story, rather than our brand, reinforces autonomy and leads to both personal and potentially collective liberation. In the vast ocean of personalities and voices within the digital information age we live in, it is important to express what might already be obvious: we weave distinct stories within the fabric of the larger social tapestry of story-making. We represent infinite personal and communal stories waiting to be experienced and told.

One way to begin is to think of yourself and your life in terms of a story. Ask yourself some of the following questions to *recognise* who you are in your story:

- How do I *perceive* myself?

- Do I *believe* this story version of myself?

- How do I *think* others perceive me? Are my perceptions of myself the same or different than the perceptions others have of me?

- Which character(s) do I *want* to be in my current story?

If the final question is unanswerable, then spend some time writing the attributes and characteristics of who you want to be, reflecting on your values, desires, and dreams.

Consider the many roles you play in your stories. Create a list of characters: son or daughter, mother or father, guide, visionary, leader, author, learner, doer, protector, creator, or lover. These descriptions can draw on your family background, relationship history, or professional experience. They can also propose new roles you may wish to play or new ways of imagining yourself.

Asking someone *What is your story?* is the same as asking them: *Who are you? What are your values?* How do you *show up* in the world? It can seem daunting to both ask and answer these questions, but it is an incredibly useful foundation for rewriting your past, current, and future stories. Let us reflect on Ben Okri's storytelling perspective:

> One way or another we are living the stories planted in us early on along the way, or we are also living the stories we planted – knowingly or unknowingly – in ourselves. We live stories that either give our lives meaning or negate it with meaninglessness. If we change the stories we live by, quite possibly we change our lives.

Because our lives are filled with fluctuating stories, the question is more concerned with *when* our stories will change rather than *if* they ever will. The trick to this process involves proactively rewriting our stories rather than having them continually written for us – a practice that stems from education and awareness leading to personal and social wellness. To build on Okri, how can we proactively write stories that give our lives meaning?

> *If life is ultimately about change and impermanence, then storytelling serves as the language of communicating that change.*

Stories make sense of our transitions and represent meaning in our lives. It all begins with us. As a result, it is valuable to become aware of the value systems from which we operate and clarify these during transformations in our families, relationships, career, health, or social groups. Return to those stories as rough drafts continually being revised.

I was recently speaking with my friend Sarah, who is in her late forties. To her dismay, she is finding some of her long-time social groups dissolving. She expressed the paradox of feeling both sadness and relief about this.

Sarah revealed that many of her friends have changed and this has shifted the values and interests in her social circles. Although she understood the fluid dynamics of social groups, she was surprised it happened with one group in particular because of its cohesiveness for over thirty years.

Sarah also acknowledged that one reason this particular group of friends fragmented is because of the increasing levels of fear they have been experiencing in their lives, and how each of them has coped with their mounting fears in middle age. Some have taken to medicating with drugs, alcohol, or pharmaceuticals, while others have shifted their political views and social values entirely, building new narratives for themselves.

Perhaps Sarah's story sounds familiar? It reflects how our stories are always changing based upon who we are at any given moment. Recognising who we are in our constantly changing stories remains an ongoing process and it is an exciting opportunity.

Embrace your stories

The second stage is more straightforward and draws on what has previously been explained in the book: *embrace* your stories by accepting that you are worthy and capable. Remember the refrain: *I am good enough.* We are all worthy just because we exist. We also all have tremendous life stories to write and rewrite in order to celebrate that existence.

How we shift our paradigm is one primary question, but another is how we *feel* in the process of transition and change. Enjoyment can be a much scarier experience than misery if joy takes us out of our comfort zone and into the unknown. The negative stories about ourselves that we have internalised limit our ability to feel adequate or even empowered.

And yet, they are familiar to us and there is a strange degree of comfort in their familiarity. Experiencing joy can take us out of familiar emotional territory if sadness has been a dominating emotion in our lives. If joy is not part of our learned stories, we often retreat back to fear, which is safer than embracing new positive feelings of well-being.

> *One of our biggest fears is learning new paradigms, which affects how we feel in the world.*

Some people have examined their fear narratives and rewritten stories that support their value and worth. But many of us have yet to achieve this. Feeling inadequate remains a constant fear if we have not yet appreciated our intrinsic value, hence the reason for the widespread impostor syndrome. One true story is that we are powerful, brilliant people. We need to reinforce and hear ourselves articulate this narrative routinely if we are to internalise it.

Begin by taking a moment and say out loud the following affirmations:

I am brilliant.

I am beautiful.

I love my body.

I am talented.

I am loved.

I am enough right in this moment.

I deserve to be alive and enjoy my life.

Now take a moment and process how you feel. What comes up for you? Is it empowering or difficult to say these affirmations out loud? Do you feel uncomfortable, embarrassed, or even a bit silly? Try to separate your somatic or emotional reaction from your rational mind, which will judge, criticise, and think this whole exercise is ridiculous.

For many of us, these self-affirmations cause anxiety, sadness, or shame because they are alien to our usual negative ways of perceiving ourselves. It is perfectly normal to feel these emotions and experiences. But it is important to know that these affirmative statements are more than just words. They can become our fundamental beliefs and be central to our new stories.

When attempting to rewrite our beliefs about our worth, a useful exercise is to speak these self-affirmations and then acknowledge what prior negative stories come up for us in response to the new story we tell about our intrinsic worth. The old fear narratives that arise might not be easy for us to acknowledge or witness. They may reinforce what we are trying to change. If so, can you see how these old fear stories are unhelpful, and can you loosen their hold on you?

The second stage of embracing is all about believing in ourselves and seeing meaning in our lives and our being – that in ourselves *we are enough*. When we are steeped in our own feelings of unworthiness, often activated by our fears, we are much less likely to live in our empowered stories. Similar to taking a new class or dating someone new, educating, empowering, and bringing ourselves to well-being through rewriting our stories presents an exciting opportunity leading to other possibilities.

If this stage becomes challenging, then surround yourself with supportive people until you believe in *you* and can embrace your preferred stories and stories that validate you. Revisit your new stories each day and practise gratitude for what they show you. Practise embracing *your* stories.

Witness the fear

The third stage brings us back to the concepts in Chapters 1 and 2 of the book: *witness* our fears and then identify the belief systems from which they arise. This step asks us to directly confront our fears. It sounds a bit terrifying, right? *I love the idea of rewriting my stories, pushing for change in my life, but I do NOT really want to uncover the fears controlling my stories.*

Consider some of your primary fear stories and the negative belief systems they sustain. Which stories do you most want to rewrite in your life? You can start small and then move to larger narratives as you feel comfortable. Do your learned fear-based narratives support what you really want for yourself and how you view yourself within your families or communities? Or, can you think about yourself differently and write a new story about the life you want?

Roger Waters, one of the founding members of the iconic band Pink Floyd, released a solo album in 2017 aptly titled *Is This the Life We Really Want?* The lyrics of the title song address the fears that align with some of our dominant belief systems:

Fear, fear drives the mills of modern man
Fear keeps us all in line
Fear of all those foreigners
Fear of all their crimes
Is this the life we really want?

The starkness of these lyrics is a salutary reminder of how dangerous it can be to entertain such false and callous ideas about other people. The question in the song is about transition, especially from living in a place of fear to one of harmony. The momentum for this change lies in our ability to decide what life we want and then to begin to write new stories to create it.

Witnessing our fears and how these are embedded in our constructed beliefs allows us to answer the question: *Is this the life we really want?* It also helps us to question what are the fears and beliefs keeping us from the life we really want. From where do these fears stem? Who is promoting these fears in society? Who is using these incitements to hate? Are they fundamental to who we are, or do they arise from a culture of fear that has written many of our stories for us that we now wish to reject or change?

Reinforce what you want

The fourth stage emphasises the outcome of our stories: *reinforce* how you want to meaningfully live your life. If we do not know what we want, and how it might improve our lives, then we cannot rewrite our stories. This might sound simple. And yet, it is not. *What if I'm judged, criticised, or blamed for expressing what I want? What if this process challenges me about what I want in my life?* Making a decision and then executing it can become a major stress and lead to feelings of fear and paralysis.

Having difficulty with identifying and requesting what we need and want is entirely understandable and commonplace. Why? Because we are taught that it is not okay to express our needs or feel worthy enough to receive them. This may arise from a common misunderstanding between *selfishness* and *self-care*. The former is often driven by fear. The latter, upon which well-being is founded, is guided by a desire for wellness and freedom in our lives.

As children, it is likely that many of us were not encouraged to positively express our needs. In school, family dynamics, or relationships, the concept of expressing our self-care needs was alien to many of us. Identifying our needs is often considered to be selfish. Even expressing legitimate wants was regarded as self-centred. But if we look at it all from another angle, we do have a duty to sustain our own self-care because failing to do so ultimately results in resentment, self-blame, or shaming others.

When other people express what they need or want, our reactions can often be judgemental because we struggle to do that for ourselves. Or, we may be intimidated by or resent those people who outwardly express themselves. If we are unable to articulate our own self-care needs, then we may be less patient or compassionate as we listen to others saying what they need. We must learn to listen to ourselves and voice our own needs if we are to be emotionally or practically available to others in need, and if we are to be empathetic and caring towards them.

Terms like *self-help* or *wellness* can activate negative responses in many of us. One likely reason is that they are terms deployed by billion-dollar industries that tacitly place blame on people for being sick or living unfulfilled lives. Many of these industries exploit vulnerability for commercial advantage. That is one part of the story.

Another possible reason many of us react negatively to wellness/self-help rhetoric is that we experience pangs of guilt as we become aware that we have not prioritised our own self-care needs. This requires attention. We need to validate self-care not as selfishness but as beneficial for everyone. Self-care and wellness are not just about caring for ourselves; they model and endorse caring for others too. In this way, we can allow space for nurturing ourselves even though it may sometimes appear selfish to others.

Living a meaningful life includes many elements, but if we cannot proactively care for ourselves, then we are often unable to achieve other aims because we simply do not have the time or energy. This presents a paradox: we know we need time to support ourselves, but we do not have time or energy to do it. The next stage teaches how to integrate what we want into our new stories of self-care.

Integrate a new story

Stage five invites us into the process of what might be called *doing* story: how we *integrate* narrative and storytelling into our lives. We always have the opportunity to create and tell our stories. To be human is to exist in story – to breathe it into our being. Our realities are constructed and narrated as stories. Regardless, we often do not think about how the pieces of story function in our lives.

The five elements of story represent universal aspects of our personal stories and those throughout human history (see Figure 11). Once we identify that we do indeed live in narrative, and consequently thrive on the language of storytelling, we can realise how fundamental it is to our knowing and being in the world. Then we can begin to change the unwanted stories controlling us.

The line between reality and fiction remains highly subjective and tentative. Magic, drawing from the Harry Potter example in Chapter 6, can manifest in many ways. Depending

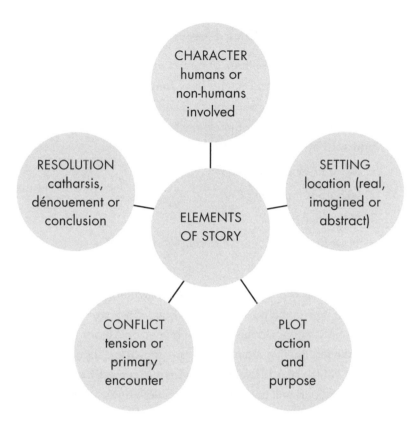

Figure 11: The five elements of story

upon one's perception and intuition, magic might be the ability to alter certain realities by changing the ways we experience and feel them in the moment.

Our wizard's wand is our ability to rewrite our stories, thereby creating a different feeling in the moment and by extension possible outcomes. Either way, our magic materialises through our ability to constantly rewrite experiences even as

STORY PRACTICE

Sit for a moment and think of one of your favourite
stories. Make sure to select a story familiar to you.
This could be a film, a novel, or a series on Netflix.
Now identify the five main elements of that story (see
Figure 11):

1. Who are the characters?
2. Where is the setting?
3. What is the plot?
4. How does conflict arise and in what forms?
5. What is the resolution?

Now think of a personal story in your own life. It could
be recent or in the past, a story of childhood, work,
or a relationship. Do the same with your own story by
pinpointing the five main elements – character, setting,
plot, conflict, and resolution. Maybe it is currently a
fear story and will contain potential challenges. If so,
what makes it difficult to recall? What belief systems are
attached to it? Is it, for example, rooted in scarcity or
oppression?

they occur. Storytelling, in other words, creates an enchanted
world beyond those limiting fear stories that had such a hold
over us in the past.

The stories we rewrite on a daily basis do not need to be
complex. In fact, they can be quite simple. A story could be *I
love my body*. It contains a *character* (me), *action* (loving), and

setting (my body). The *conflict* rests in my struggle to love my body and the *resolution* arises in my acceptance of loving my body completely. Why? The *I love my body* story represents a rewritten version of a common fear story in consumer culture: *I hate my body.*

The rewrite of this mini-story contains all five elements. Many of our daily stories will look just like that. The simpler and more direct stories remain the most challenging because they are both the most common and debilitating for us. This is how our fear stories function. They are usually not elaborate narratives with plot twists, character betrayal, and a reckoning – although sometimes they are! Rather, they are simple fear narratives through our lives that have become embedded in our thinking. Here are some common examples:

I am a failure.

I am inadequate.

I am an impostor.

If I quit my job, even though I hate it, I will be homeless.

If I leave this relationship, I will never meet anyone again.

What I do in the world has no value.

Fear stories are not usually complicated in construction. The complexity comes from how they are ingrained in us. I have yet to meet many people who do not consciously or unconsciously think *I am inadequate* at least once a day. It represents one of the most common human fear narratives. The rewrite is simple in application but difficult in practice: *I am perfectly adequate in this moment.*

Stories traditionally have a subject and action. When rewriting our own stories, we are often the subject. Then we can begin to ask ourselves additional questions:

- What is the action required in relation to the purpose or problem?

- Are there other characters involved?

- How complex is my fear story?

- Does the setting/location have any bearing on the action relating to my fear?

Drawing on the story of *I love my body*, we could even include more detail in it. Here is an example of a story from my friend Angela. When casually chatting about how our bodies are ageing, she openly shared the following:

> *My body has changed in my life since I was in my early twenties. I feel shame about my weight gain after having two children and hitting middle age. Despite still feeling healthy, I don't like how I look. Because of my body, I feel unlovable. I'm not sexy or desirable. The truth is that I hate my body right now and I fear this will only get worse as I get older.*

This is a common story even if we shift the gender, age, or other specifics about the changing body. The fact is, many of us struggle to love our bodies in a consumerist culture that constantly sells the option of a better, perfect, and ultimately impossible body. The *poor body-image* belief systems run deep in this story, so it takes patience to rewrite over time. Here is one immediate rewrite to start the process of integrating:

Although my body is different now than when I was in my early twenties, I like the way I feel. I am proud of this body which has brought two children into the world. I am different now and I can wear different types of clothes. I also feel sexier because I know who I am in my own body. I feel elegant and beautiful right in this moment. I'm learning how to love my body.

The next few drafts might depend upon how often this story is rewritten. Transition and change are part of the process. Building upon the first five stages of the REWRITE process, the aim is to think of our challenges in terms of stories that are constantly changing.

- *Recognise* who you are in the story (Character)
- *Embrace* the story (Setting)
- *Witness* the fear and beliefs that are attached to it (Conflict)
- *Reinforce* what you want, such as the outcome or a feeling (Plot)
- *Integrate* a different story supporting your well-being (Resolution)

By rewriting the story of our bodies, we begin a process of change, even if it might take time to concretise variations of this story. Analysing and constructing the story serves as an important element, but another quite powerful aspect of REWRITE is telling our stories to ourselves and others.

Tell this story

Stage six asks us to *tell* the rewritten story to ourselves, and others, until it becomes integrated. Repeat the story over and over in order to believe it. Make it part of you. Give it voice.

In addition to telling the story to yourself, also find audiences with whom you can practise your storytelling. Rewiring our beliefs comes from practice. Rewriting our stories is an important step, but the crowning achievement remains believing our stories. Over time, witnessing, telling, and living our stories changes the chemistry of our brains.

Drawing on two decades of extensive research, the neuroscientist and author Dr Paul Zak found that telling stories elicits responses in audiences that increase their capacity to empathise and connect with other people. The release of the naturally occurring chemical oxytocin increases our capacity for empathy. The result is obvious: it improves the world we live in. Referring back to the research referenced in Chapter 9 about narrative empathy, we can see how both digesting and telling stories develops empathy, producing personal and social change.

Whether we are consuming a novel, a binge-worthy television show, a podcast, or listening to a friend's story, we can increase our range of empathy and understanding. For instance, we can practise this when meeting a friend for coffee or when we come home from work. Instead of beginning a conversation with stories of hardship, tell each other two positive stories that have happened since you last spoke.

My partner and I often practise this at night. I ask, 'Can you tell me about a story you have rewritten today?' She knows the REWRITE lingo already, so we can jump right into the storying process.

Telling our stories contributes to the wellspring of our social narratives, counteracting some of the negative dominant belief systems and establishing more generative ones for ourselves in the future. Stories are designed to be told to others, so find encouraging audiences at home, work, or online. The key here is to find people who support and believe in you. Practise on them first until the new stories are ingrained. Telling our stories strengthens our creativity and the resolve that is fundamental to enhancing our storytelling.

Enhance your creativity

The final stage encourages building one of the most important tools in the practice of REWRITE. To *enhance* your creativity is to cultivate curiosity and wonder, and to allow space for stories to develop and mature. Despite how organised we try to be, our lives are subject to continual mystery and ultimate possibility.

Fully experiencing life's transformational opportunities requires creative tools that are often sidelined in our everyday lives. Just as athletes need to constantly train to maintain top physical form, we need to access our creativity to maintain top storytelling form. Enhancing creativity serves as the energy source which powers the entire process. Living a creative life heightens our ability to imagine other possible stories.

But here is a catch: creativity can also contain traces of fear for many of us. Even our stories about creativity might hold beliefs rooted in fear, particularly in a culture of conformity which limits our creative potential. To create is to risk failing, being wrong, or feeling judged. It presents a scary prospect for many of us because it incites vulnerability – putting ourselves out there for potential criticism.

Creativity can appear in the most unlikely places. Living a creative life does not necessarily involve publishing books, exhibiting our paintings in galleries, or performing music on stage, although any of these activities might be involved. We can all find undertakings that fuel our creative yearning.

In fact, a wide range of actions or experiences could be considered creative outside of the typical classifications. Creativity can occur in even the most ordinary and mundane activities. It is not the activity *per se* but how it is undertaken that distinguishes the ordinary from the creative. From kite-flying to knitting, canoeing to cooking, it is the energy, curiosity and novelty we bring to what we do that makes it creative.

One of the common stories about creativity is that we are either born creative or not. As an author and educator, I have heard the same essentialist belief about writing: you are either born a writer or not. This either/or split is not only a false fear story and oppositional concept, but also an ingrained belief system. It is an untruth that influences an enormous number of people who consequently ignore their creative potential. The real story is that everyone has an aptitude and need for creativity.

In their book *Wired to Create: Unravelling the mysteries of the creative mind*, cognitive psychologist Dr Scott Barry Kaufman and *Huffington Post* journalist Carolyn Gregoire argue that we are all 'wired to create'. Our lives present all sorts of opportunities to exercise and express our creative potential. As the authors explain, creative 'self-expression' serves as a powerful way of dealing with inevitable challenges in our lives.

Despite biases to the contrary, perpetuated through various belief systems supporting social conformity, we all 'display creativity in many different ways'.

The American author Elizabeth Gilbert also points out insightfully in her book *Big Magic: Creative living beyond fear* that creativity is about curiosity. It is less about producing a product and more about being in the process. Gilbert's definition of creativity speaks to the social judgements and criticisms attached to narratives of fear.

She defines creativity not as 'pursuing a life that is professionally or exclusively devoted to the arts', but rather 'living a life that is driven more strongly by curiosity than by fear'. Fear and curiosity, just like fear and creativity, might appear at opposite ends of the spectrum. But, in reality, they are integral to each other, two sides of the same coin for many of us.

We cannot experience curiosity without feeling fear, because the creative process, or being curiously artistic, requires that we undergo uncertainty – to jump across a chasm without knowing how far it is to the other side (or if another side even exists). Gilbert reminds us that we 'are not required to save the world' with our creativity. And, I would also add, by cultivating our creativity, we *can* and *do* save the world one person at a time. Without being a requirement, it nevertheless is an indirect result.

Returning to what Gilbert simply refers to as 'creative living', it would seem that this phrase reduces the perceived grandeur of creativity to the everyday (in the best way possible). Rather than becoming a concert pianist or painting like Picasso, we can engage in small activities that will enrich our creative living, with noticeable benefit. Creativity drives our sense of wonder and possibility, building a fundamental bridge towards recreating our stories and supporting our well-being.

> *Creativity makes the impossible possible.*

Allow me to illustrate a personal example of how this process is not as scary as it may seem. My aunt Marsha took painting and drawing classes when she was a child. She later stopped when she became a mother. Years after her children became adults, Marsha wanted something to spark her curiosity and inspiration. After considering many options, she decided to take up painting and drawing again.

For Marsha, the intent was never to become a famous painter. She wanted to find an activity that ignited her interest and passion, enhancing the quality of feeling inspired as she grew older. Even though she started classes again, she continued with her normal life: living with her husband in retirement, seeing friends, visiting grandchildren, and attending church events. In the meantime, her painting activities prospered.

After several years, Marsha created a website showcasing some of her paintings; she displayed her work at exhibitions, and she even won several awards. These outcomes, while fantastic, were never the aim, nor did they motivate her process. They manifested and eventually flourished because she began to cultivate some of her creative aspirations.

I am happy to report that embracing a creative practice later in life did not tempt Marsha to drink IPAs with hipsters at the local micro-brew pub, smoke hand-rolled cigarettes, live out of her VW van, or any other regressive activity we might associate with the *creative soul* archetype.

We all have the capacity to embrace and grow our creativity. Like worthiness, creativity is a birthright. We already have it. Our fear of creativity based upon extreme stereotypes of what it means to live a creative life is sometimes what prevents us from exploring the places where creativity can thrive.

This last stage of REWRITE – to *enhance* your creativity – is what supports the modalities of living creatively. Creativity, supported by intuition, necessitates letting go and surrendering into the moment of our storying process. Being human is to be experimental with our lives, to create experiences and opportunities every day in our work, relationships, and ourselves.

Allowing fear to dominate is what impedes this process. The paradox is that creativity and all that comes with it reduces our fear. We can surrender to the process of creativity, releasing our fears, in order to design our stories.

The poet and songwriter Leonard Cohen memorably wrote: 'You lose your grip, and then you slip / Into the masterpiece'. Consider surrendering enough to 'slip' into the masterpiece of your creation, whether it is cooking dinner for your family or painting a watercolour for yourself. Then, the impossible becomes possible.

Incorporating more storytelling into our lives changes how we feel in each moment and enhances our sense of possibility and well-being. The seven stages of REWRITE provide a template through which to build our story archive by replacing fear stories rooted in unwanted constructed belief systems. REWRITE can be used as outlined in this book or in tandem with other effective forms of education, narratively inspired models of therapy, or coaching that supports ways of using narrative tools as primary devices for enhancing our physical, mental, or spiritual well-being.

Try exploring REWRITE on a daily basis until it becomes ingrained and eventually replaces the majority of your fear narratives with other stories. The results can be life-changing.

REFLECTION QUESTIONS

Can you think of situations in life where you rely on storytelling? Perhaps when spending time with friends, family, or in work settings.

Can you think of a current fear story in your life, whether it be small or large? Use the process of REWRITE (see also the chart in the Appendix). Write it down as you go. Assess how you feel. Then practise on another fear story tomorrow. Try this for a week on several different stories. Make whatever modifications are necessary. What parts of REWRITE are the most difficult to apply? Why?

CHAPTER 11

Inviting Stories
of Gratitude

The power of thanks

A lot of ground has been covered so far. The journey began by acknowledging our social and personal patterned stories rooted in a culture of fear. We then explored how we might reframe how to perceive the world as a paradigm shift by questioning damaging belief systems and their persistence in the sociocultural context. Next, we turned to understanding how stories remain fundamental to human history and existence, as well as to our own lives on a moment-by-moment basis. Finally, drawing on all of this background, we arrived at the place of using pragmatic tools to assist the process of REWRITE.

This brings the book to a close and also, hopefully, to the beginning of the path of rewriting our stories to achieve further education, empowerment, and well-being for ourselves and in our sociocultural surroundings. This concluding chapter focuses on gratitude as a final piece in the rewriting process. Ending with another useful technique grounded in gratitude practice will not only aid the process of rewriting stories, but also immediately assist in improving our lives. Similar to intuition and creativity, gratitude contains immense power to support our storying process.

> *Gratitude rewires our system, shifting our perception and ways of seeing the world, and changes how we experience every day.*

Practising gratitude involves many variants and is different for everyone. We are all free to explore and use this practice as it pertains to our own lives. For some, it might be spending

INVITING STORIES OF GRATITUDE

time in the garden while being wholly aware of that experience. For others, it might be vocalising affirmations each day as a meditation practice. Or, as a variation, it could be acknowledging gratitude throughout the day both internally to ourselves and externally to others.

Before I start my day, for example, I express my gratitude for whatever strikes me in that moment. Here is a sample list of what I might affirm:

I am grateful for my health and for being alive.

I am grateful for having enough food and for living in relative safety.

I am grateful for the sun pouring through the windows.

I am grateful for feeling loved.

I am grateful for feeling at peace.

I am grateful for feeling joy.

I am grateful for all of the opportunities and possibilities in my life.

I am grateful for this day that I have in front of me.

On any given day, I express these same affirmations of gratitude, along with some additions depending on my mood. Sometimes I declare them out loud and sometimes silently. Even though it only takes a couple of minutes, this process has transformative effects.

Why is this seemingly simple practice so effective? 'Thank you', according to the author Alice Walker, 'is the best prayer that anyone could say. I say that one a lot. Thank you expresses extreme gratitude, humility, understanding.' Gratitude is a daily practice where we take the time to acknowledge the good, the positive elements in our lives that occur for every one of us no matter how bad things may seem. It provides space to not only say or think 'thank you', but also to feel and embody it – integrating it into our being.

Even on my worst days, that might otherwise feel stressful, I can still witness a blossoming cherry tree flowering on my walk to work. I feel deep gratitude for these simple experiences. These moments are gifts. See and witness them in your own life. They are everywhere in abundance and entirely free to access.

Benefits of gratitude

Related to our learning process set out in this book, gratitude serves as one of the most potent antidotes to fear. Why? Because it rewires how we function each day. One of the aims of this book is to practise rewriting our stories and particularly those rooted in fear, providing us with autonomy and freedom to experience greater well-being in our lives. But what if we arrived at a point where we could simply live from a place of gratitude without having to constantly rewrite our fear stories?

Besides my own attempt to extol the benefits of practising gratitude, medical and psychological research has confirmed countless physical and mental health positives:

- Reduces stress and tension

- Increases patience, humility, and empathy

- Enhances quality sleep (reducing insomnia)

- Improves immunity

- Generates serotonin and dopamine (naturally occurring chemicals in our bodies that increase joy and happiness)

- Lowers cholesterol

- Eases depression

- Heightens energy levels and productivity.

Health educator and nutritionist Dr Paula Szloboda explains that the more we practise gratitude, the more we normalise it and integrate it into our lives. The effects are immediate. We complain less and have less fear and anxiety. As a result, we feel happier and more energised.

Some other benefits relate to what has been discussed throughout the book, particularly in relation to offsetting what fear can do to our bodies (see Chapter 2). For instance, practising gratitude also does the following:

- Challenges old belief systems and supports new ones

- Reduces overthinking

- Enhances intuition and creativity

- Increases conscious perception

- Boosts self-worth and compassion for others

- Cultivates awareness

- Spotlights the present moment

- Develops resiliency and courage

- Generates empowerment.

The obvious takeaway is that practising gratitude serves as an accessible and inexpensive way to significantly increase the quality of our lives and reduce the prevalence of fear in our daily existence.

Addressing old fear stories is inevitably challenging, as is the process of writing new ones, until they become more ingrained. But practising gratitude, along with cultivating creativity, can begin immediately and can support the processes explained throughout this book. If you can incorporate just one practical tool from this book, it would be to develop a gratitude practice for about one to five minutes each day.

Once I started practising gratitude, I quickly realised how often I complain – about other people, myself, traffic, my job, food, politics, or whatever else. It is easy to fall into this irritable pattern. While a good venting session releases tension, constant complaining causes more stress, tension, and fear.

We must not forget that complaining is part of our social conditioning. We are taught to criticise everyone and every-thing, which ultimately comes from our acquired beliefs about our own inadequacy. A culture of fear thrives on producing a scapegoat – an *enemy* or *other* to complain about. A culture of lack rooted in scarcity emphasises deficit rather than promot-ing affirmation and abundance.

How do we remedy this pattern? Witness the moments of complaining. When they begin, simply rewrite the story in that moment to one of gratitude. Here is a common example:

Complaint story

My boss is power hungry and totally incompetent. I can't stand him. Because of him, I hate going to work each day.

Gratitude story

I appreciate that I have autonomy in my job. I'm glad the walk to work each day gives me energy and allows time for exercise and listening to podcasts. Because my supervisor struggles to perform his job, it opens up unique opportunities for me to assist in larger projects at work, taking on exciting new roles.

This process does not ignore or negate the poor behaviour of the supervisor. Rather, it shifts our perception of how we should emotionally and physically feel in the moment. We can find gratitude in many situations. Retelling stories about a difficult supervisor only ignites our fears and anxieties, making us feel worse and typically preventing any future change. We can instead simply rewrite this story through gratitude. Throughout the gratitude practice, we may realise, for example, that quitting a particular job is the best outcome for us.

There is nothing complicated about gratitude, and yet it is extraordinary. Its value rests in its simplicity and applicability in our everyday lives. Perhaps Brené Brown sums it up best when she states: 'I don't have to chase extraordinary moments to find happiness – it's right in front of me if I'm paying attention and practicing gratitude.'

Similar to the availability of gratitude in our lives, our stories also appear right in front of us if we pay attention. The stories we do not want to be a part of will become more apparent the more we practise gratitude and identify what we want. Our gratitude practice can both catalyse and motivate our rewriting process.

One story ends, another begins

Some of the monumental issues our world is facing right now demand the cultivation of more compassion, empathy, and gratitude. The planet remains a collective place, where almost eight billion people must learn to live with one another and trillions of other species and organisms (e.g. animals, plants, insects) in an increasingly smaller space. Pandemics of the scale of COVID-19 make us all aware of how interconnected we are regardless of where we live in the world. Despite personal, social, and political attempts to isolate and divide people and communities, we must live and connect with each other in order to promote both personal and collective welfare.

The poet and author David Whyte effectively describes how gratitude can affect our entire planet:

Gratitude is the understanding that many millions of things come together and live together and mesh together and breathe together in order for us to take even one more breath of air, that the underlying gift of life and incarnation as a living, participating human being is a privilege; that we are miraculously, part of something, rather than nothing.

Our stories intertwine and become interdependent whether we want them to or not. This is the theatre of the human drama and we all have a part in the play. We all belong to 'something'; that is the storied privilege of our existence.

My own observation is that we are currently transitioning on a global scale in an attempt to change our story from one of fear and division to one of collectivity and compassion. Perhaps this seems a bit optimistic considering current events of rising authoritarianism, pandemics, ecological breakdown, and political division. Using history as a guide, humans usually only change when faced with adversity. Regardless, I have been inspired by all the people – with an even greater representation of youth populations – rising up in the face of adversity, oppression, and discrimination.

Rather than business as usual, people seem to have had enough of greed, hate, violence, patriarchy, and global warming. While the momentum shift among many populations around the globe may not reflect the current political or economic agendas in specific countries, it nevertheless persists and grows with fierce tenacity.

> We are in a crisis of rewriting our global story. Who will write our new story, and will it be one of fear and isolation or one of solidarity and interconnection?

When I watch news, listen to people, or feel the collective energy of the world, I observe most people going about their daily lives wanting economic fairness, racial equality, clean air to breathe, freedom to love who they wish, compassion and assistance for those who are in need, and a sustainable world for their children to inherit.

It is easy to fall into the fear stories currently circulating. Fortunately, there are also gratitude stories that greatly out-number the fear narratives. We must look for and then build upon them. We must use our storytelling magic to change these fear narratives. We are currently undergoing monumental change. This shift begins and builds momentum by rewriting our personal and collective stories.

Teachers of all political persuasions are demanding liveable wages and budgets to support student learning. Students are insisting on safety from violence at schools. People are pushing for gender and sexual orientation equity in all sectors of society. Youth are voting for change at historic rates. Divergent religious communities are coming together in the face of collective tragedy. Black Lives Matter has become a global movement supported by many different cultures calling an end to racially motivated oppression and police violence. People are protesting the pollution of drinking water and air, so much so that children are going to court, as well as speaking out publicly, to fight for an environmentally sustainable future.

These are only some of the many social stories being rewritten right now. They are rooted in our personal stories of transformation and transmitted on a social scale. The stories we write become part of a larger global human narrative that is being rewritten.

It begins with global communities. It begins with local communities. It begins with you. Your role matters. Each of us changes the collective future in some way. We are all Hummingbird.

Developing gratitude necessitates seeing the beauty in ourselves and other people. After a month or two of practising gratitude, try something new. What I am about to suggest might seem shocking, but it will increase your gratitude even further: spend quality time with people similar to you *and* with people different from you. Rather than disagree with them, just listen to their stories. Rather than *believing in* something or someone, try *believing with* them. Using your observational intelligence, hold space for difference without judgement or criticism.

Or, going even deeper, find areas of convergence. Seek connection. See what happens. Most of us just want to be seen and heard. We all just want to be loved, but often find ourselves in the wrong story. Try to see other stories in people, even if they are not as relatable to your lived experience.

This is where self-care and social-care build on each other to empower collectivity in society. They intertwine and interconnect, shaping interrelationships and intersection. There is no *self* without the *social*, regardless of how much we isolate ourselves from each other.

Climate change remains a social issue that impacts individuals as well as the entire world. Racism erodes an entire society, not only the victims. Patriarchy creates a world of competition and inequality that erodes society and affects everyone, including those benefiting from unequal power structures. We are all interdependent and rely upon our comparative stories to grow.

Reducing a culture of fear happens when we shift the narrative. Fear thrives and expands in isolation, separation, and silos. As outlined in chapters 4 to 7, fear infiltrates our social systems where we are all conditioned to remain separated and fear the *other*, or an enemy, who we can blame for our problems.

What if we had gratitude for these other people? What if we had gratitude for ourselves at the same time? As we rewrite our own stories, what if part of those stories expressed gratitude for difficult neighbours, co-workers, ex-bosses, or ex-spouses?

The author and spiritual teacher Carlos Castañeda talked about acknowledging the challenging *gifts* in our life to promote change, what he called *petty tyrants* – or people who infuriate us, the 'button-pushers' who 'throw things off-balance'. At the same time, petty tyrants are also our teachers because they force us to monitor our 'own reactions and habitual behaviors'. They indirectly help us discover value in our current and future stories, and finding gratitude for them is part of our progression. Other people, especially those outside of our realm of experience and understanding, are integral to our stories.

When one story ends, another begins. We are ending one human story and beginning another, a larger story with many sub-stories containing the potential to change the paradigm as we know it.

This process begins with hundreds, thousands, and millions of people deciding to take the leap, to seek empowerment and well-being despite the chaos around them, and to contribute to recreating our sociocultural contexts and systems as life-affirming. The way to do this is to understand how much we live in story, which remains changeable, dynamic, and empowering.

Change the world one story at a time.

We have that power.

As a collective.

As a person.

REWRITE...

REWRITE Your Story

Recognise who you are

What are your stories and which belief systems guide them?

Embrace your stories

How can you accept and validate your stories?

Witness the fear

How do you witness fears and clarify belief systems tied to them?

Reinforce what you want

What are your goals and processes to achieve them?

Integrate a new story

Can you create new stories that ultimately empower you?

Tell this story to yourself and others

How can you communicate empowering versions of your stories?

Enhance your creativity

How can you cultivate creative tools for storytelling?

GLOSSARY

The following brief definitions correspond with terms used in the book. Depending upon the context or specific uses, many of the definitions are more extensive. Please consult outside sources for further explanation.

Binary opposition
Words or concepts that are defined through their opposite meaning more than the word or concept itself.

Cartesian dualism
A concept by the seventeenth-century French philosopher René Descartes that proposed that the function of the mind and body are separate, rather than interconnected and reliant upon each other.

Catastrophising
The process of imagining the worst outcome when presented with many possibilities.

Conscious perception
The ability to perceive the world through conscious observation and awareness, drawing on multiple forms of intelligence and knowledge systems.

Education
The formal and informal process of producing and embodying knowledge.

Empowerment
Building strength, confidence, or solidarity through individual or collective growth or action.

Epistemology
The study of knowledge and ways of knowing and believing.

Fear
A biological, psychological, and/or emotional response to both real and perceived threats.

Future-making
The process of creating, constructing, and producing our personal and social futures.

Intuition
Perceiving or accessing information beyond the rational intelligence, particularly through emotions, perceptions, or sensations that influence decisions, behaviours, or actions.

Metaphor
Using figurative language to explain objects or actions in an image or story. Unlike a simile that uses literal comparison (the giraffe is *like* a tree), metaphor uses an imagined comparison (the giraffe *is* a tree).

Narrative
Accounts of particular events often communicated through writing, speaking, or imagination. Another term for story.

Narrative coaching
Supporting individuals and groups through a process that explores narratives within a larger sociocultural context, leading to further education, empowerment, and well-being.

Narrative empathy
The process of producing and/or experiencing empathy through stories and storytelling.

Neoliberalism
A particular phase of capitalism that serves as an ideology as much as an economic theory, positioning competition as a defining factor of human relationships, while also subsidising private wealth through public funding.

Ontology
The philosophical study of *being* – how humans relate to and understand becoming, existence, and reality.

Oppression
Systematic and prolonged control of groups or peoples to attain or hold power, often involving cruel or unjust treatment. Oppression can also be produced through socially constructed language and ideology.

Patterned (or learned) beliefs
Constructed beliefs, or ways of seeing the world, that have been learned or inherited through the patterned systems in which people live, such as in society, government, or religion.

Relational / Relationality
Living in relationship to other people as interconnected beings rather than as isolated individuals.

Self-care
The process of improving a person's mental, emotional, spiritual, or physical health in relationship to the collective.

Social construction
Considers all knowledge and experience to be learned or *constructed* through social beliefs, customs, norms, interactions, and/or relationships that create and define societies.

Story-making
The process of generating individual or collective stories through forms of co-creation.

Storytelling
The process of conveying or sharing stories through language, sound, writing, acting, actions, or images.

Unity of opposites
Both separate and interconnected at the same time, existing precisely because of their inherent tension and attraction of opposition. The Chinese Yin/Yang symbol and the waxing and waning cycles of the moon are two examples.

Well-being
A state of being for individuals or groups supporting positive

conditions often relating to health, happiness, meaning, and prosperity.

Zeitgeist
Drawn from eighteenth-century German philosophy meaning 'spirit of the age', it indicates moments in history that are specific to cultural ideas or beliefs.

Zero-sum game
In game and economic theory, this term refers to a situation where one player's gain is the other player's loss – implying only two options exist: winning or losing.

OTHER RESOURCES

This information about services and supports, across public and voluntary sectors, has been compiled for readers, with particular emphasis on resources relevant to this book. However, the directory cannot be, nor does it claim to be, comprehensive, and further information about international or regional services may be obtained through websites.

In providing this list, no personal recommendation with regard to the services listed is made or implied by the author or by the publishers. While every effort has been made to ensure that the information given is accurate and up-to-date, no responsibility can be taken in the event of errors.

Additionally, it is always recommended that in any situation of concern people seek professional advice, and in relation to health or mental health that they consult their local general practitioner or health authority.

American Psychological Association: **www.apa.org**
(Professional association for psychologists in the United States)

Aware: **www.aware.ie**
(Information and support on fear, anxiety, and depression)

British Psychological Society: **www.bps.org.uk**
(A representative body for psychologists in the United Kingdom)

Canadian Psychological Association: **www.cpa.ca**
(The primary organisation representing psychologists throughout Canada)

Change your story, change your life:
www.cbc.ca/player/play/2676829160
(Interview with Professor Timothy Wilson about stories that frame our lives)

Dulwich Centre: **www.dulwichcentre.com.au**
(A gateway to narrative therapy and community work)

The Emotion Machine: **www.theemotionmachine.com**
(Website and database for psychology and self-improvement)

European Federation of Psychologists' Associations:
www.efpa.eu
(Umbrella organisation for European psychological associations)

Family Therapy Association of Ireland:
www.familytherapyireland.com
(Information on therapy for individuals, couples, and families)

The Happier Human: **www.happierhuman.com**
(Self-care website with articles on gratitude)

Irish Association for Counselling and Psychotherapy:
www.iacp.ie
(Professional association for counsellors and psychotherapists)

Irish Feminist Network: **www.irishfeministnetwork.org**
(Information and support on gender equality)

Men's Development Network: **www.mens-network.net**
(Support for men seeking personal and social change)

Mental Health Ireland: **www.mentalhealthireland.ie**
(Advocacy and support for mental health)

MindReading Project:
www.ucd.ie/medicine/capsych/mindreading/
(University College Dublin resource linking literature with
mental well-being)

MindYourSelf Series: **mindyourselfbooks.ie**
(Safe, researched, peer-reviewed self-care, health and well-
being book series)

Ministry of Stories: **www.ministryofstories.org**
(Writing and mentoring education centre spearheaded by
author Nick Hornby)

Narrative 4: **www.narrative4.com**
(Global network of authors, educators, and students focused
on story)

National LGBT Federation (NXF): **www.nxf.ie**
(Information and support for LGBTQ communities)

Psychological Society of Ireland:
www.psychologicalsociety.ie
(Professional body for psychologists and psychology in the
Republic of Ireland)

Story Center: **www.storycenter.org**
(Organisation transforming lives and communities through stories)

Story Wars: **www.storywars.net**
(Digital platform for collaborative story-making)

Taos Institute: **www.taosinstitute.net**
(Organisation advancing social constructionist ideas and practices)

The Truth About Stories: **https://www.cbc.ca/radio/ideas/the-2003-cbc-massey-lectures-the-truth-about-stories-a-native-narrative-1.2946870**
(Indigenous author and professor Thomas King at the Massey lecture series)

Vancouver School for Narrative Therapy:
www.vancouverschoolfornarrativetherapy.com
(Teaches narrative therapy practices on non-individualism, social justice, feminist, queer, and post-colonial topics)

OTHER READING

The concepts in this book reflect the author's years of teaching, mentoring, and leading classes, workshops, and individuals. Topics and reflections are also based upon the author's research, as well as research findings from other sources. The following readings, while not exhaustive, serve as references in the book, as well as suggestions for further reading.

Ackerman, D., *A Natural History of the Senses* (New York: Vintage, 1990)

Bakhtin, M., *The Dialogic Imagination*, ed. and trans. Michael Holquist (Austin: University of Texas Press, 2008)

Blair, L., 'How to Stop Catastrophising: An expert's guide', *The Guardian*, 29 December 2017, https://www.theguardian.com/lifeandstyle/2017/dec/29/stop-catastrophising-expert-guide-psychologist

Blake, W., *The Marriage of Heaven and Hell* (Oxford: Oxford University Press, 1975)

Bourke, J., *Fear: A cultural history* (London: Virago, 2007)

Brown, B., *Daring Greatly: How the courage to be vulnerable transforms the way we live, love, parent, and lead* (New York: Avery, 2012)

— *Rising Strong: How the ability to reset transforms the way we live, love, parent, and lead* (New York: Random House, 2017)

— *The Gifts of Imperfection: Let go of who you think you're supposed to be and embrace who you are* (Center City, MN: Hazelden, 2010)

Butler, J., *Gender Trouble: Feminism and the subversion of identity* (New York: Routledge, 2006)

Capra, F., *The Tao of Physics: An exploration of the parallels between modern physics and Eastern mysticism*, 5th edn (Boulder, CO: Shambhala, 2010)

Chandna, D., 'The Cure Is Not in the Pill Bottle', TEDxMontrealWomen, 8 February 2017, https://www. youtube.com/watch?v=hL4IxADUjvM

Clandinin, D.J., *Engaging in Narrative Inquiry* (New York: Routledge, 2018)

— and Connelly, F.M., *Narrative Inquiry: Experience and Story in Qualitative Research* (New York: Wiley, 2004)

Coelho, P., *The Pilgrimage: A contemporary quest for ancient wisdom*, trans. Alan R. Clarke (New York: HarperCollins, 2009)

Cooperrider, D.L. and Whitney, D., *Appreciate Inquiry: A Positive Revolution in Change* (Oakland, CA: Berrett-Koehler Publishers, 2005)

Cytowic, R.E., 'The Pit in Your Stomach Is Actually Your Second Brain', *Psychology Today*, 17 January 2017, https://www.psychologytoday.com/ca/blog/the-fallible-mind/201701/the-pit-in-your-stomach-is-actually-your-second-brain

Emmons, R.A. and Mishra, A., 'Why Gratitude Enhances Well-Being: What we know, what we need to know', in K.M. Sheldon, T.B. Kashdan and M.F. Steger (eds), *Designing Positive Psychology* (Oxford: Oxford University Press, 2011)

Foucault, M., *Power/Knowledge* (New York: Vintage, 1980)

Freire, P., *Pedagogy of the Oppressed* (Harmondsworth: Penguin, 1972)

Garrison, A., 'Antianxiety Drugs – Often More Deadly Than Opioids – Are Fuelling the Next Drug Crisis in the US', *Modern Medicine CNBC*, 3 August 2018, https://www.cnbc.com/2018/08/02/antianxiety-drugs-fuel-the-next-deadly-drug-crisis-in-us.html

Gergen, K., *An Invitation to Social Construction*, 2nd edn (London: Sage, 2009)

— *Relational Being: Beyond self and community* (Oxford: Oxford University Press, 2009)

Gergen, K.J. and Gergen, M.M., 'Narrative Form and the Construction of Psychological Science', in T.R. Sarbin (ed.), *The Storied Nature of Human Conduct* (New York: Praeger, 1986), pp. 22–44

Gershon, M., *The Second Brain* (New York: HarperCollins, 1999)

Gilbert, E., *Big Magic: Creative living beyond fear* (New York: Riverhead, 2015)

Goleman, D., *Emotional Intelligence: Why it can matter more than IQ* (New York: Random House, 2005)

Gottshcall, J., *The Storytelling Animal: How stories make us human* (New York: Mariner Books, 2013)

hooks, bell, *Teaching Community: A pedagogy of hope* (New York: Routledge, 2003)

— *Yearning: Race, gender, and cultural politics* (Boston: South End Press, 1990)

Iacoboni, M., *Mirroring People: The science of empathy and how we connect with others* (New York: Picador, 2008)

Kaufman, S.B., 'What Would Happen if Everyone Truly Believed Everything Is One?', *Scientific American*, 8 October 2018, https://blogs.scientificamerican.com/beautiful-minds/what-would-happen-if-everyone-truly-believed-everything-is-one/

— and Gregoire, C., *Wired to Create: Unraveling the mysteries of the creative mind* (New York: Perigee, 2015)

Keen, S., 'A Theory of Narrative Empathy', *Narrative*, vol. 14, no. 3, 2006, pp. 207–36

King, T., *The Truth About Stories: A native narrative* (Toronto: Anansi Press, 2002)

Kripal, J., *The Flip: Epiphanies of mind and the future of knowledge* (New York: Bellevue Literary Press, 2019)

Lakoff, G. and Johnson, M., *Metaphors We Live By* (Chicago: University of Chicago Press, 1980)

Lopez, B., 'Interview', *Poets and Writers*, vol. 22, no. 2, 1994

Madigan, S., *Narrative Therapy* (Washington, DC: American Psychological Association, 2011)

Maté, G., *In the Realm of Hungry Ghosts: Close encounters with addiction* (Toronto: Random House, 2008)

Monbiot, G., *Out of the Wreckage: A new politics for an age of crisis* (London: Verso, 2017)

Morrison, T., 'No Place for Self-Pity, No Room for Fear', *The Nation*, 150th Anniversary Special Issue, 6 April 2015, https://www.thenation.com/article/no-place-self-pity-no-room-fear/

Nancy, J.L. and Engelmann, P., *Democracy and Community*, trans. Wieland Hoban (London: Polity, 2015)

Okri, B., *A Way of Being Free* (London: Head of Zeus, 2014)

Orloff, J., *The Ecstasy of Surrender: 12 surprising ways letting go can empower your life* (New York: Harmony Books, 2014)

Pullman, P., *Daemon Voices: On stories and storytelling* (New York: Knopf, 2018)

Rankin, L., *The Fear Cure: Cultivating courage as medicine for the body, mind, and soul* (Carlsbad, USA: Hay House, 2015)

Ruiz, M., *The Four Agreements: A Toltec wisdom book* (San Rafael, USA: Amber-Allen Publishing, 1997)

Rumi, *The Essential Rumi*, trans. Coleman Barks (New York: HarperCollins, 1995)

Rushdie, S., *Luka and the Fire of Life: A novel* (New York: Random House, 2011)

Salmon, C., *Storytelling: Bewitching the modern mind*, trans. David Macey (London: Verso, 2010)

Sarbin, T.R. (ed.), *Narrative Psychology: The storied nature of human conduct* (New York: Praeger, 1986), pp. 139–49

Smith, D., 'It's Still the "Age of Anxiety". Or Is It?', *The New York Times*, 14 January 2012, https://opinionator.blogs.nytimes.com/2012/01/14/its-still-the-age-of-anxiety-or-is-it/

Szloboda, P., 'Gratitude Practices: A key to resiliency, well-being & happiness', *Beginnings*, vol. 28, no. 1, 2008, pp. 6–7

Tolle, E., *The Power of Now: A guide to spiritual enlightenment* (Vancouver: Namaste Publishing, 1999)

Tomm, K. and Govier, T., 'Acknowledgement: Its significance for reconciliation and well-being', in C. Flaskas, I. McCarthy and J. Sheehan (eds), *Hope and Despair in Narrative and Family Therapy: Adversity, forgiveness and reconciliation* (New York: Routledge 2007)

Vostroknutov, A., Polonio, L. and Coricelli, G., 'Observational Learning and Intelligence', USC-INET Research Paper, no. 17-05, 2017, pp. 1–34

Wagamese, R., *Embers: One Ojibway's meditations* (Madera Park, BC: Douglas & McIntyre, 2016)

Weber, M., *The Protestant Ethic and the Spirit of Capitalism*, trans. Talcott Parsons (New York: Charles Scribner's Sons, 1958)

White, M. & Epston, D., *Narrative Means to Therapeutic Ends* (New York: Norton, 1990)

Whitney, D., Miller, C.A., Teller, T.C., Ogawa, M., Cocciolone, J., León de la Barra, A., Moon, H., Koh, A., and Britton, K., *Thriving Women Thriving World: An Invitation to Dialogue, Healing, and Inspired Actions* (Taos, NM: Taos Institute Publications, 2019)

— , Rader, K., and Trosten-Bloom, A., *Appreciative Leadership: Focus on What Works to Drive Winning Performance and Build a Thriving Organization* (New York: McGraw-Hill Education, 2010)

Whyte, D., *Consolations: The solace, nourishment and underlying meaning of everyday words* (Langley, USA: Many Rivers Press, 2015)

Wilson, T., *Redirect: Changing the stories we live by* (New York: Little, Brown, 2015)

Yahgulanaas, M.N., *Flight of the Hummingbird: A parable for the environment* (Vancouver: Greystone Books, 2008)

Yunkaporta, T., *Sand Talk: How Indigenous thinking can save the world* (New York: Harper One, 2020)

Zak, P.J., 'Storytelling: Changing the world one brain at a time', *My Weber Media*, 9 November 2017, http://signpost.mywebermedia.com/2017/11/09/storytelling-changing-the-world-one-brain-at-a-time/

— 'Why Inspiring Stories Make Us React: The neuroscience of narrative', *Cerebrum*, no. 2, 2015, https://www.ncbi.nlm.nih.gov/pmc/articles/PMC4445577

— 'Why Your Brain Loves Good Storytelling', *Harvard Business Review*, 28 October 2014, https://hbr.org/2014/10/why-your-brain-loves-good-storytelling

Zeidner, M., Matthews, G. and Roberts, R.D., *What We Know about Emotional Intelligence: How it affects learning, work, relationships, and our mental health* (Cambridge, MA: MIT Press, 2009)

INDEX